CHARLESTON

ARCHITECTURE
AND INTERIORS

CHARLESTON

ARCHITECTURE
AND INTERIORS

SUSAN SULLY

PHOTOGRAPHS BY THE AUTHOR

Gibbs Smith, Publisher
TO ENRICH AND INSPIRE HUMANKIND
Salt Lake City | Charleston | Santa Fe | Santa Barbara

First Edition
11 10 09 08 07   5 4 3 2 1

Published by
Gibbs Smith, Publisher
P.O. Box 667
Layton, Utah 84041

Orders: 1.800.835.4993
www.gibbs-smith.com

Designed by Laura Milton
Printed and bound in Hong Kong

Library of Congress Cataloging-in-Publication Data

Sully, Susan.
  Charleston architecture and interiors / written and photographed by Susan Sully.—1st ed.
    p. cm.
  ISBN-13: 978-0-941711-92-0
  ISBN-10: 0-9-41711-92-7
  1. Architecture, Domestic—South Carolina—Charleston. 2. Interior architecture—South
Carolina—Charleston. 3. Interior decoration—South Carolina—Charleston. 4. Charleston (S.C.)—
Buildings, structures, etc. I. Title.

NA7238.C3S85 2007
745.09757'915—dc22
                              2007011272

[Charleston's] climate, the southern habits, the social arrangements, all give a picturesqueness in their separate ways, and there is a fine air of age, and dusty decay which invests whole streets with the venerableness of the past.—It is like Italy in the feeling that belongs to it,—and ought to have painters and poets.

—Charles Eliot Norton, 1855

This book is dedicated to the people of Charleston who, throughout the centuries, have created, preserved, and reinterpreted a city of exquisite and incomparable grace.

CONTENTS

When I wrote my first book about Charleston, *Charleston Style: Past and Present* (1999), I had just recently moved to Charleston and become entranced by its old-world beauty and the way the past infused the present. That volume celebrated the spirit of Charleston, and as a newcomer to Charleston, I was delighted to discover that the book captured the hearts of many old Charlestonians. Having lived in Charleston for a decade now, I have never ceased to be fascinated by the city, its homes, and people. During this time, I have witnessed a stirring of the old city not unlike the revival called the Charleston Renaissance, which occurred in the first decades of the twentieth century.

Now, as then, people are drawn from afar to the city's rarified grace and charm, and to its trove of refined architecture and decorative arts. They are collecting its houses as last vestiges of a time of grace and beauty, when the finest artisans pooled their resources to create dwellings that were both elegant and extremely livable. These new owners inhabit these houses in a spirit of mingled reverence and ingenuity, restoring the architectural remnants of the past while infusing the rooms and the structures with a mind toward modern living, comfort, and style. Charlestonians and other southerners are also at the heart of this renaissance, redefining the city's style from the inside out—ever mindful of the past but filled with a spirit of the new.

Witnessing this, I have come to recognize Charleston style as something that is not only distinct and definable, but also fluid and evolving. Each period of great wealth and influx of residents, from the seventeenth century to the present, has brought new influences of taste. Modern aesthetics have come in with the tides, yet they have always been softened, muted, and blended to become part of Charleston itself. Perhaps it is the result of the semitropical climate, where everything must submit to the effects of heat, sun, and humidity. Perhaps it is the enduring influence of the city's first founders, English colonists who left an indelible legacy of Anglophilic elegance. Or perhaps it is the history of the place, a city that formed deep allegiances to the Old South where moonlight and magnolias, gardenias and Earl Grey tea still hold sway.

The city's dwellings, whether museum houses and old family homes or newly settled ones, just recently filled with furnishings and decorative objects, share certain ineffable qualities. I decided to write this book, *Charleston Architecture and Interiors*, in an attempt to identify these elements. To do this, I've explored three categories: historic Charleston, eclectic Charleston, and quintessential Charleston. In the first, I've looked at houses that reveal Charleston style at its various zeniths of aesthetic expression. In the second, I've explored houses which, in their mix of styles and ingredients, express something uniquely regional about Charleston. In the third, I tried to capture certain qualities that transcend style to express the very essence of the city and its people.

I hope that this book will serve not only as an informal study of the city's architectural and decorative expressions, but also as a source of inspiration to those who are moving to Charleston or who wish to capture a bit of its charm in their own homes, wherever they live. I write this book not only as a celebration, but also as an invitation to come and be a part of timeless Charleston.

ACKNOWLEDGMENTS

No book can exist without the generosity of many people. I could not have created *Charleston Architecture and Interiors* without the advice, talents, and assistance of many people. It is impossible to name them all, but in addition to all the homeowners who have allowed me into their houses as I have researched, written, and photographed this book, I would like to thank:

Pete Wyrick and Christopher Robbins
of Gibbs Smith, Publisher

Jonathan Poston, author of *The Buildings of Charleston* (University of South Carolina Press, 1997)

Robert P. Stockton, author of several unpublished house histories concerning dwellings in this book

Carroll Ann Bowers, Valerie Perry, and Steve Hanson of Historic Charleston Foundation

Tracy Todd, Mary Edna Sullivan, and Barbara Doyle of Middleton Place

Randall Goldman of Patrick Properties

Professional Color Service, Metairie, Louisiana

INTRODUCTION

Every city has a distinct design identity. The older the city, the more complex this identity becomes. Sometimes, the architecture of an old city that has seen a lot of history pass by seems to suffer from a kind of style schizophrenia, with multiple identities expressing themselves distinctly upon its facades and within its rooms. New Orleans, with its French, Spanish, Caribbean, English, and American influences, comes to mind as such a place. Key West is another, with its surprising mélange of New England, Bahamian, Southern, and early-twentieth-century American styles coexisting within the compact old-town area.

Founded in 1670, Charleston, South Carolina is one of America's oldest cities and one that had all the right ingredients for the development of a complex and somewhat incoherent regional style. Flourishing as the crown jewel of England's royal colony of Carolina, the city was one of America's wealthiest and most opulent from the late seventeenth century to the mid-nineteenth. The get-rich-quick opportunities it offered attracted immigrants from England, Ireland, Scotland, France, and Germany who all brought their own regional style personalities with them. Over the seventeenth to the twenty-first century, Charleston has defined itself first as a British colonial capital; then an American city during the Revolution; a Southern city during the Civil War and Reconstruction; and finally, purely Charleston. Unique and charming, alternately dreamy and bustling, the city's streets are unlike any other in the country or the world. Surprisingly, the design identity that evolved out of this mix of people, events, and elements is almost completely unified—an enduring regional style that blends its disparate influences and ingredi-

ents into a harmonious, coherent whole. Even as Charleston's residents have shifted in taste every few decades, moving through phases of Georgian, Federal (or Adamesque), and Greek Revival styles, their houses and collections of furniture and objéts seemed to retain something irrefutably distinct through the centuries.

When you walk into a Charleston home, whether it retains its eighteenth-century shape and style or has been dramatically remodeled, whether it is packed with family heirlooms or sparely decorated with carefully chosen accoutrements, more often than not, you feel in the marrow of your bones that you are in Charleston. A glimpse of blue-and-white china, a dark gleam of mahogany, the silhouette of a column, the scent of jasmine, a frayed edge of old velvet or the luster of new silk-satin—these combine in a distinctly recognizable domestic style.

ANGLOPHILIA, CLASSICISM, AND CHINOISERIE

The unity of Charleston's style in architecture, furniture, and decorative arts can be attributed in part to the city's long-standing Anglophilia. Founded by the British Lords Proprietors in 1670 and populated primarily by English colonists, the city had a strong political and social connection with England for two centuries. Most of its wealthy citizens in the seventeenth and eighteenth century were either born in England or were connected through family ties or trade with England. They traveled back and forth across the Atlantic; ordered furnishings from England or from local cabinetmakers who imitated British styles; bought silver and tableware in England (or France and Ireland, just as their British cousins did); and emulated British trends in their architecture and domestic arrangements. While their architecture was modified better to suit Charleston's semi-tropical climate, the proportions, room arrangements, and decorations typically mirrored fashionable English trends.

By the eighteenth century, English tastemakers had adopted two major sources of style inspiration that were to continue influencing architecture, furniture, and the other decorative arts for two centuries. Georgian England was obsessed with Classical architecture, modeling both residential and public buildings upon the temples of Greece and Rome and the villas of sixteenth-century Italian architect, Andrea Palladio, who revived these sacred forms and interpreted them for residential purposes. While Georgian massiveness and restraint gave way to Adamesque and Regency delicacy in the late eighteenth and early nineteenth centuries, the designers-du-jour, including Robert and James Adam, George Hepplewhite, and Thomas Sheraton, still looked to classical Greece and Rome for inspiration.

The second major design influence that permeated British style from the seventeenth through the nineteenth and even into the present century, is Asian style. English merchants began traveling to and trading with China late in the seventeenth century. They brought back textiles, artworks, ceramics, and furniture that became status objects in wealthy homes. Before long, the influence of these objects infiltrated British-made design, as demonstrated in the Chinese designs of Thomas Chippendale and the adoption of chinoiserie throughout all aspects of British design. As the word "chinoiserie" suggests, French tastemakers also played an important role in popularizing Chinese style, adopting Chinese (and Japanese) color schemes and motifs in their porcelains, textiles, and decorative objects.

Other influences came and went in England, continental Europe, and Charleston, including the English "Gothick," the French Baroque and Rococo, and even Egyptian styles. But these tended to sublimate themselves beneath the supremacy of neoclassical and Asian influences, offering pleasing

grace notes of variation within a unified approach to design. Whether looking at a late-eighteenth-century Georgian residence, an early-nineteenth-century Federal one, or a mid-nineteenth-century Greek Revival style home in Charleston, one can find distinct similarities in the vocabulary of columns, door and window surrounds, cornice moldings and ceiling medallions, all borrowed from Greek and Rome. The furnishings that occupy these rooms are equally infused with a Classical spirit and an occasional Chinese detail, whether a linen press inlaid with garlands drawn from Greek and Roman monuments or a chair with square Chinese legs.

Although Charleston, like other American cities, separated itself politically from England following the Revolution, it maintained closer trade ties to its mother country than any other American city. While other Southern cities, including Savannah and New Orleans, began to trade more directly with American centers of industry, including New York and Philadelphia, Charleston continued to buy and sell most frequently with England. Because its cabinetmakers so deftly imitated English styles, Charleston-made furniture was often mistaken for the work of English master craftsmen, wrongly attributed throughout most of the late nineteenth and twentieth centuries. When Charlestonians did begin to purchase the furniture that New York and Philadelphia shipped in quantity to the city in the early nineteenth century, they typically bought objects that resembled English prototypes.

SOUTHERN ACCENTS
While Charleston's Anglophilia played a central role in shaping the city's seventeenth-, eighteenth- and early-nineteenth-century tastes, the Civil War and its aftermath directed its evolution from the late nineteenth century to the present. As the economic and trade issues that sparked the conflict grew more heated in mid-nineteenth

century, prominent Charlestonians continued to cling to England. Despite increasing pressure from the federal government to break its trading patterns, Charleston led the fight to protect the practice of shipping agricultural products abroad in return for British goods and money. In an effort to protect their traditional way of life and commerce, Charlestonians were among the first southerners to sign the Ordinance of Secession. The first and last shots of the Civil War were fired in Charleston, and their echoes rang loudly for a century after the war ended.

During the decades following the Civil War, when other Southern cities sought to redefine themselves as centers of the New South, embracing industry, trade with New England, and popular American styles of architecture such as the Second Empire (modeled after a French style) and the Romanesque Revival, Charleston clung to the past. As it relates to the city's decorative arts, this clinging reflected not only political and social isolationism, but also financial realities. Because of the active role its citizens had played in commencing the Civil War, and the city's recalcitrance during the war (as compared to other southern cities that surrendered more readily), Charleston was the victim of punitive post-war policies.

During the second half of the nineteenth century, Charleston languished as other port and manufacturing centers, including Atlanta, Birmingham, Savannah, and New Orleans, flourished. Little money was available to finance the construction of new buildings and the remodeling or refurnishing of old ones. There were some exceptions and, as a result, downtown Charleston is lightly peppered with mansard roofs and Victorian brackets and ball-and-spindle work. But the greater part of Charlestonians just held on tightly to the remains of the city's golden age—the decaying buildings,

the collections of cherished furniture and decorative objects, the marble statuary of their overgrown gardens. Living proudly amidst the ruins, surrounded by objects that took on the patina of age and genteel decay, continuing social rituals that spoke of a wealthier past, they forged their own distinct and charming way of life.

THE BIRTH OF ECLECTICISM

The hallmark of this formative period of Charleston style is eclecticism. While wealthy Charlestonians of previous eras could afford to build new houses and redecorate old ones in styles modeled on the changing tastes of England and post-Revolutionary America, post–Civil War Charlestonians could not. This explains a certain sameness that defined Charleston interiors from the 1860s to the 1960s, which shared the hallmarks of traditionalism and eclecticism. Such houses were typically decorated with a mismatched collection of eighteenth- and nineteenth-century British and American furniture, what English silver was not sold to pay Reconstruction-era taxes, the ubiquitous blue and white Canton Chinese export ware that was shipped to the city by the boatload, and faded curtains of silk or chintz with Chinese patterns. As present-day Charleston architect Randolph Martz once said, "Charlestonians didn't 'decorate'. . . they lived with their possessions, their mementos, souvenirs, and debris."

A SENSE OF PLACE

To this enforced eclecticism, Charlestonians brought the magic of their pride and their gracious way of living. They transformed their dependence upon vestiges of former glory into a fierce spirit of preservation, protecting their august architecture from destruction when other American cities embraced urban renewal, tearing down old buildings and destroying antique urban plans. They defined their own brand of Southern charm, casting an enchanting spell by surrounding themselves and visitors with antique objects infused with personal histories and walled gardens overflowing with fragrant blooms.

Late-nineteenth-, twentieth-, and twenty-first-century Charlestonians redefined elegance to suit their situation. For them, elegance no longer required new and fashionable accoutrements. Rather, it was fashioned from tasteful combinations of antiques that complemented one another in shape, form, and hue. Stylistic restraint was celebrated over riotous displays of wealth. To these elements, Charlestonians also brought romance, as defined in post-industrial England—a longing for the unattainable ideal and nostalgia for a disappearing way of life rooted in an agrarian culture.

Romancing their past by surrounding themselves with objects that whispered of a golden age of wealth and glamour, Charlestonians created one of the most romantic cities in America. During the early twentieth century, artists and writers flocked to Charleston in a movement that became known as the Charleston Renaissance, celebrating the anachronistic ways and quaint decrepitude of the city. And Charleston opened its doors and garden gates, letting the curiosity seekers admire the beguiling way of life its citizens had forged out of centuries of mercurial history.

Whether sharing their homes and gardens with friends in familiar cycles of social interchange or opening them to strangers, Charlestonians displayed their penchant for hospitality. Houses that were designed for conviviality, with cool gardens, breezy piazzas (as they call porches), and large drawing rooms, continued to fulfill the function of hospitality. And Charleston style became recognized as something unique, precious, and infinitely desirable.

Tourists have frequented Charleston from the early twentieth century to the present, and their contributions have helped fuel the economic recovery that swept the city in the last half century. Today, travel and design magazines routinely feature Charleston on their covers and in their pages. Charleston-made furniture has finally taken its place among the most highly prized—and priced—antiques. New residents are buying up old homes south of Broad Street, and new preservation initiatives are being offered to encourage the protection of these houses' interior details and their surrounding gardens.

While continuing to protect their decorative past, Charlestonians (both new and old) are also participating in the continued evolution of Charleston style. Embracing the elements that define this regional design personality, they are updating the style. Just as the city's golden age residents often remodeled their homes, embracing new trends in architecture, so some of these inhabitants are integrating aspects of modern design into old homes. And yet, even as they purchase new furniture and art, they also adhere to the principles of post–Civil War Charleston style, mixing these ingredients with British and American antiques, Asian elements, and an air of old-world elegance and southern charm.

This is Charleston—a place where layers of history coexist harmoniously to create a style identity rich in variety, yet curiously unified. In the pages of this book, readers will recognize similar objects decorating rooms that are found in historic house museums and homes decorated by today's most fashionable interior designers. They will find that the same design impulses inform houses inhabited by families who have lived in Charleston for centuries and by newcomers. They will discover the enduring strands of taste, and habit, and heart that define timeless Charleston.

FROM JACOBEAN
TO GEORGIAN STYLE

MIDDLETON PLACE
A Historic House Museum and Garden

The Middletons are one of Charleston's oldest and
finest families, representing the values and tastes
of four centuries of colonial English, revolutionary
American, and Southern life. Henry Middleton,
who acquired the large plot of land that he transformed into Middleton Place in 1741, was the son
of an English family who came to the Carolina
colony via Barbados, where they and their fellow
colonials amassed fortunes in the sugar trade. Proud
representatives of the British crown, these colonists relished their English roots and modeled their
New World lives upon the styles favored by their
wealthy relations across the sea.

The house that Henry Middleton acquired along
with the property upon his marriage to Mary
Williams, was designed in a hybrid of Georgian
and Jacobean tastes that reflected early-eighteenth-
century English country house designs. In overall
plan, the large brick mansion, built sometime
before 1741, reveals an early Georgian influence. In
particular, its rectilinear symmetry and center-hall
plan is reminiscent of Georgian England's preoccupation with the severely elegant country villas
designed by Italy's foremost seventeenth-century
architect, Andrea Palladio. A description published
one hundred years after the house's construction
describes its "beauty and elegance" as "nearer, than
any place I have seen, in America, to the Italian
villas . . . near Rome."

While the primary facades of classic Georgian era
villas typically boasted temple-like pediments and

colonnades, however, Middleton Place's western façade was decorated with a narrow, three-story tower. Designed in a Jacobean manner that hearkens to a style popular in the late seventeenth and early eighteenth centuries, this detail suggests that the owner of this New World house nurtured ties to an old England that pre-dated Georgian modishness. When Henry Middleton had two identical outbuildings, or flankers, constructed to the north and south of the main building in 1755, he commissioned these in a purer expression of Georgian style, which was by then in full flower on both sides of the Atlantic. One was designed as a gentlemen's guest wing, the other as a conservatory and library for Henry's collection of thousands of books.

Of all three buildings, only the southern flanker still stands, the others having been demolished by the combined effects of war, fire, and earthquake. It is interesting to note that when Henry's great-grandson Williams Middleton restored this building, he added curvilinear baroque gables also reminiscent of the country architecture of Jacobean England. Today, this compound of buildings inspired by the architecture of seventeenth- and eighteenth-century Europe and England stands in varying states of rescue and ruin amid a landscaped garden whose design draws from even earlier sources, the late-seventeenth-century formal gardens of France and the sixteenth-century Italian gardens and ancient Roman prototypes that inspired them.

Although the name of Middleton Place's landscape designer is lost to history, it is assumed that he was English, and that he modeled the garden according to the precepts of André Le Nôtre, creator of Louis XIV's gardens of the Palace of Versailles. The elegant geometry of the overall plan, the sweeping lines of tree-lined allées, and orderly forms of parterre gardens all comply with Le Nôtre's logical,

Age-of-Enlightenment approach to design. They also reflect the axial geometry of ancient Roman gardens and temple grounds that inspired Le Nôtre.

While these elements reveal the tendency of mid-eighteenth-century Charlestonians to look over the Atlantic and back through time for aesthetic inspiration, there is much about Middleton Place and the lives of its residents that is rooted firmly in New World soil. Henry Middleton was the second president of the First Continental Congress, and his son, Arthur, was a signer of the Declaration of Independence. While this father and son forged American ideals of democracy and freedom, the next two generations of Middletons helped shape Southern history. Henry's grandson, also named Henry, was a governor of South Carolina, and his son, Williams, a signer of the Ordinance of Secession. These generations of Middletons also changed the face of the Southern landscape, planting some of the region's first camellias and azaleas—brilliantly flowering plants now considered synonymous with the South.

PREVIOUS PAGE (seen through trees): The surviving flanker can be glimpsed through the dense stands of old azaleas that grow on a bluff of the Ashley River. A springhouse stands on the edge of a creek that was flooded to create a pool powering the plantation's rice mill.

OPPOSITE: Precisely arranged paths form pleasing geometric compositions while drawing the eye to the grandeur of the natural setting, including giant oak trees and the gently bending river.

TOP LEFT: Well pruned parterres of boxwood enclose rectangles of green lawn that fall away to reveal river views. Reflecting the geometric approach to landscape design favored by seventeenth-century French architect, André Le Nôtre, the garden's design was adapted to suit the specifics of the site along the Ashley River.

BOTTOM LEFT: Wide allées and a shimmering canal planted with azaleas and dogwoods form the triangular axes that give Middleton Place gardens their geometric plan. Within this overall plan, lesser allées and polygonal gardens provide hours of idle strolling in which to enjoy the plantation's man-made and natural beauty.

OPPOSITE: Viewed from the moon bridge that crosses the Rice Mill Pond, a wall of ancient dogwood trees woven with vines of wisteria forms a painterly composition.

Thanks to the diligence of subsequent generations of the family, the gardens at Middleton Place still look today much as they did at the time of the mid-eighteenth century, before the ravages of time and war took their toll. But no amount of effort could prevent the walls of Henry Middleton's grand mansion from collapsing after being first torched by Union troops, then felled by the great earthquake of 1886. However, the dedicated efforts of present-day Middleton descendant Charles Duell have resulted in the transformation of a surviving outbuilding into a house museum where many Middleton family treasures are exhibited. Scattered across the country in the years following the Civil War, this collection of paintings, furniture, and decorative objects testifies to a century of connoisseurship that traces the evolution of American taste.

Although the flanker, built as a gentlemen's guest wing, boasts few interior embellishments of the architectural kind, its elegant accoutrements still recall the refined lifestyle enjoyed by the pre–Civil War residents of Middleton Place. Family portraits painted by Jeremiah Theus, Benjamin West, and Thomas Sully grace the walls, depicting generations of Middletons characterized by an air of genteel intelligence. A drop-leaf breakfast table carved with square Chinese-style legs and fluid fretwork attributed to Thomas Elfe attests to the genius of late-eighteenth-century Charleston furniture makers, who emulated popular English styles. Similar tables designed by Thomas Chippendale can be found in English country houses and city homes of the same era on the other side of the sea.

In contrast, the furniture of the flanker's music room is nearly all made in Philadelphia, denoting a shift in buying practices that occurred in the early nineteenth century when northern furniture workshops, including Duncan Phyfe's, flooded Charleston's market. While the room's furniture is American, its artwork and decorative objects nearly all hail from continental Europe, where Charlestonians enjoying the Grand Tour often shopped for easily portable objéts.

A French Aubusson carpet covers the floor, its rich ruby tones reflected in a collection of Bohemian glass from Central Europe. A painting by Greuze (or possibly a contemporaneous copy) depicting a girl with fingers in her ears hangs on the wall—a witty choice of subject for a room devoted to musical entertainments. One of the most interesting paintings in the room is a copy by Guérin of Gérard's portrait of Madame Récamier, a leading member of society in early-nineteenth-century France, who entertained John Izard Middleton (son of Arthur) at her famous Paris salons. This painting reveals the close ties uniting revolutionary-era American and French intellectuals.

The flanker's dining room offers an equally intriguing survey of early American tastes. The room's early-nineteenth-century table is made in the style of New York's best-known cabinetmaker, Ducan Phyfe. The mahogany chairs that surround it, though made in America, emulate the shield-back designs popularized by late-eighteenth-century London furniture designer, George Hepplewhite.

TOP LEFT: Fourth-generation Middleton, Williams Middleton, continued his grandfather's and great-grandfather's passion for landscape architecture and botany, planting this naturalistic garden of azaleas along the Rice Mill Pond in the mid-nineteenth century.

TOP MIDDLE: Throughout Middleton Place gardens, perfect cones and precise lines of boxwood contrast pleasingly with the sinuous silhouettes of gnarled oak trees and the undulating river.

TOP RIGHT: Cultivated by French horticulturalist André Michaux, some of the camellias at Middleton Place are among the first grown on American soil.

OPPOSITE: A nineteenth-century Italian marble statue of cherubs playing instruments graces a secret garden at the end of an allée lined with camellias and shaded by oak trees. Similar to the Italian sculpture that dotted the eighteenth-century garden, this sculpture was given to Middleton Place Foundation as part of the garden's late-twentieth-century restoration.

ABOVE: This Empire style sofa, circa 1820, was probably made in Philadelphia. The curving lines of its arms imitate the shape of a lyre. An early note found in the Middleton family's papers indicates that this red silk and gold damask upholstery is original, dating from the sofa's purchase by Williams and Susan Middleton.

OPPOSITE: Many of the Middleton ladies excelled at the musical arts. This room celebrates the refined pastime with an English mahogany music stand holding a piece of sheet music given to Catherine, daughter of Henry Middleton, when he was ambassador to Russia. Philadelphia-made furniture fills the room and French and Italian paintings cover the walls.

The epergne, the candlesticks, and the wine coasters were all made in England, purchased by Arthur Middleton and his wife Mary during a long visit in the late 1760s and early 1770s. While Charlestonians tended to purchase their silver in London, they set their tables with porcelain from England, France, and China. Pieces from all three countries are represented in the Middleton Place collection of Bourbon Sprig—a pattern that originated in Paris during the reign of Queen Marie Antoinette.

While these rooms reveal a cosmopolitan taste shared by wealthy Americans of both southern and northern regions, the summer bedroom upstairs offers a glimpse into purely southern style. While the winter bedroom down the hall is cloaked with a silk carpet and lined curtains and bed hangings of toile, this room is an airy retreat fashioned to maximize comfort in the region's hottest season. Typically, Charlestonians stored away their fine textiles in the summer, covering their floors with rush mats less vulnerable to sun and insect damage, and curtaining windows with light cotton dimity. Headboards were removed from beds that were hung with mosquito netting and pushed to the center of rooms to best benefit from cross-breezes. In these ways, southerners who were unable to remove to cooler climates (the Middletons summered in Newport, Rhode Island up to the mid-nineteenth century) endeavored to weather the summer as comfortably as possible.

In 1865, Union soldiers occupied Middleton Place, ransacking the plantation's buildings and burning them. What priceless paintings, books, and furniture were not burned or strewn about the ground were "liberated" by Union troops and officers. Among these was an early-nineteenth-century landscape now hanging in the dining room, which a Union medical officer claimed to have taken for "safekeeping" during the war. It, along with several other paintings, was finally returned to Middleton descendants after ten years of correspondence.

For a half century following the war, Middleton Place's brick residences, plantation outbuildings, and landscaped gardens succumbed to decay, becoming a landscape of ruin and tangled neglect that vividly symbolized the Old South's moribund economy

and post-war mood. But beginning in the 1920s, a new generation of Middletons returned to the place, renovating the surviving flanker as their home and beginning the monumental task of restoring the gardens. The present-day descendant has transformed the beautifully restored gardens and buildings of Middleton Place into a museum property that was named a National Historic Landmark in 1972. Open to visitors from morning until dusk every day of the year, Middleton Place testifies to the enduring dreams of the region's first and finest families, inviting any willing visitor to partake of their New World grandeur and Old South style.

ABOVE: A gravy boat with a lion head and a graceful, footed compote both share the Bourbon Sprig pattern favored by the Middleton family, a china pattern popularized in Paris during the reign of Marie Antoinette.

TOP RIGHT: A portrait by renowned American artist Thomas Sully of his sister, Elizabeth Sully Smith, wife of Henry Middleton Smith, hangs upon the wall of the dining room. Fine American furniture fills this room, including a Federal style breakfront, circa 1800, and an early-nineteenth-century American table in the New York style of Duncan Phyfe.

BOTTOM RIGHT: Hepplewhite-style chairs flank a fine breakfront bookcase of inlaid mahogany attributed to Edmund Johnson of Salem, Massachusetts. Like his Charleston contemporaries, Johnson emulated the refined neoclassical styles of England's finest cabinet-makers in this masterpiece of design.

TOP LEFT: This fine carved chair, made between 1740 and 1750 by an unknown English or Irish cabinetmaker, reveals the far-reaching influence of English designer, Thomas Chippendale. Once owned by the Drayton family of neighboring Drayton Hall, this chair has nearly identical twins in the collections of the Nathaniel Russell House and Heyward-Washington House in downtown Charleston.

TOP RIGHT: The summer bedroom's centerpiece is a circa 1800 mahogany rice bed, so named because its posts are decorated with carvings of rice sheaths. Characteristic of Charleston plantation design, these beds feature removable headboards, which allow for better cross-ventilation during the hottest summer months. This room also features an English slant-top desk and English chest-on-chest, both dating from the turn of the eighteenth century.

OPPOSITE: This late-eighteenth-century clothes press, with its architectonic pediment, was made circa 1790 by a Charleston cabinetmaker. Such monumental pieces of furniture were common in the homes of well-to-do Charlestonians, who stored their folded clothing in their drawers. Opulent silk waistcoats and breeches belonging to Henry Middleton and his son, Arthur, are still stored in this press's sliding drawers.

GEORGIAN GRANDEUR

THE BRANFORD-HORRY HOUSE
The Home of Laura and Steve Gates

The Branford-Horry House, built circa 1755, is one of Charleston's most imposing Georgian residences in more ways than one. Rising three stories high and standing five bays wide, the massive masonry dwelling addresses Meeting Street with a monumental two-story piazza that projects over the sidewalk, causing anyone who walks by to pass quite literally in its shadow. Although this piazza was added after 1826 and reflects the neoclassical tastes of Federal-period owner, Elias Horry, its dignity and massing is utterly compatible with the scale and design of the Georgian façade built by Horry's grandfather, William Branford.

Branford was one of the Carolina colony's most successful planters, and the house he built for his second wife, Elizabeth Savage, was one of the grandest Charleston residences of the period. The interior moldings, carved primarily from cypress, are considered among the finest in Charleston and America and reflect the Georgian era's preoccupation with the designs of sixteenth-century Italian architect Andrea Palladio. Palladio, in turn, borrowed architectural shapes and decorative motifs from ancient Greece and Rome, inventing a style that emphasized a highly refined sense of proportion, a formal approach to surface decoration, and an impressive, weighty sense of scale.

Grand entertaining rooms fill two of the three stories of the Branford-Horry house, each lined with original cypress paneling and crowned with cornices carved with the egg-and-dart, dentil, or Greek key patterns favored in the era. The ground

PREVIOUS PAGE: This classic Georgian double house, built circa 1755, acquired a Charleston-style piazza in the early nineteenth century. Massive proportions and neoclassical details, including both Doric and Ionic capitals upon the columns, unite this Federal detail with the Georgian edifice.

TOP LEFT: Hand-painted in China, the silk wall coverings in the stair hall were custom made by the English company de Gournay to fit the hall's irregularly shaped surfaces. The antique golden tone of the background complements the pale ochre shade of the painted cypress wainscoting, while the colorful foreground informed the palettes of rooms opening off the hallway.

BOTTOM LEFT: Silk upholstery in muted pastel tones and the whimsical shapes of shell-backed chairs and a contemporary painting of a rose-colored gown create a light-hearted mood in the first-floor drawing room. French, English, and American furniture and artwork blend easily in the comfortable proportions of the cypress-paneled chamber.

OPPOSITE: A Regency sofa with lyre-shaped arms and a caned back lends delicate grace to the first-floor drawing room. Designer Amelia Handegan selected yellow silk taffeta with pink iridescence for its upholstery. The pink cushion is made from the same fabric turned inside out.

floor's primary entertaining rooms are arranged on either side of a wide center hall and a long drawing room runs across the front of the second floor, terminating in a small withdrawing room. These rooms have served a variety of purposes over the centuries in which the house has been inhabited, but their appearance has been nearly unaltered. The present residents have placed easements upon them to insure that they stay as they are for future generations.

The most significant interior change was wrought in the 1820s by Elias Horry, who, in addition to adding the piazza, also widened the doors opening into the two ground-floor entertaining rooms and added door surrounds echoing the neoclassical shapes of the piazza. It is interesting to consider that Elias's father, Thomas Horry, who lived in the house during the Revolutionary War, vacillated between allegiance to the English and Patriot causes, ultimately rejecting the Crown in favor of the new republic. So the house has vacillated over the ensuing years between stylistic expressions of English and American tastes, marrying quintessential Georgian form and ornamentation with Federal-style applied detail, including the piazza and the hall door surrounds.

Present-day owners Laura and Steve Gates, who have lived in both England and America and love both Georgian and Federal style architecture, were immediately captivated by the house. "I just walked in and decided this was the place," recalls Steve. The couple wanted a residence that would be large enough to hold large house parties of family and friends. With a third floor accommodating four bedrooms in addition to two more on the second floor, the house met that need. Although the entertaining rooms are quite formal in appearance, their intimate scale balance that formality, creating spaces that lend themselves to comfort as well as elegance.

"The proportions of the rooms are so perfect that when you are in them, you totally relax," Laura comments. "It doesn't matter what your day has been like and what has happened to you. When you walk in the front door and into the proportions of the house, all the tension and stress of the day melts away." When the Gates hired Charleston-based interior designer Amelia Handegan, Laura asked her to help create a décor that was warm and inviting. The resulting interior combines eighteenth-, nineteenth-, and twenty-first-century furnishings that blend late Georgian and early Federal style with contemporary comfort.

To set the tone for the elegantly eclectic interior, Handegan suggested hand-painted silk wallpaper from the English company de Gournay for the stair hall. Its chinoiserie pattern of birds and vegetation recalls the influence of French rococo design in the late Georgian period, when such wall coverings were popular. Laura chose this over Zuber wallpaper because the painted silk's golden ochre tone gave it an antique appearance that complemented the architectural setting. While adding grace notes of delicately rendered flora and fauna, the silk's pink, yellow, green, and blue tones established the palette for lustrous upholstery used throughout the ground-floor entertaining rooms.

OPPOSITE: The dining room is a study of harmonious contrast, with the informality of the seagrass rug and slip-covered and skirted chairs offset by the elegance of the Italian giltwood chandelier and Chippendale armchairs. The German baroque angel and contemporary English still life span centuries, yet complement each other perfectly.

OPPOSITE: The Gates have placed interior easements on this and the other main rooms of the house in order to protect the exceptional Georgian paneling and moldings from future change. The second-floor drawing room's palette is inspired by colors found in the vibrant Heriz carpet on the floor. Antique Chinese tomb figures and bird prints by Audubon further enliven the space.

TOP LEFT: The paneling and moldings of the second-floor drawing room are considered some of the finest of their type in America. Deeply beveled panels of cypress surround the mantel, where several decorative motifs are carved in a variety of woods including tulipwood and mahogany.

TOP MIDDLE: The curvilinear shape of an eighteenth-century French armchair complements the shell-like form of an Italianate chair with a pink silk taffeta seat.

TOP RIGHT: The brilliant tangerine shade of this guest bedroom is in keeping with the Georgian taste for highly colored walls. Striped canopies embellish a pair of French empire beds, visually diminishing the distance between them and the room's high ceiling.

In the first floor drawing room, a pair of French armchairs upholstered in blue-gray silk, a Regency caned sofa with silk cushions in yellow and pink, and a pair of shell-backed chairs reminiscent of rococo design cluster in informal seating areas. An Oushak carpet with shades of chartreuse, pink, and gray unfurls across a seagrass mat, blending formal and informal floor coverings. A mixed-media painting by contemporary artist Todd Murphy hangs on the cream-colored cypress paneling, the rosy shades of a woman's gown glowing through a layer of glazed Plexiglas. Also sharing the room are a portrait of eighteenth-century English artist Joshua Reynolds and a genre painting by nineteenth-century American artist Thomas Sully.

The interior designer chose a seagrass mat for the dining room floor, juxtaposing its rough texture with shimmering gold silk curtains and the gleam of an Italian giltwood and crystal chandelier. A pair of Chippendale armchairs with square Chinese style legs and a "Gothick" tracery back recalls the tastes of Georgian England, while the room's artwork spans the centuries, with a baroque period carved wooden angel from Germany facing a twenty-first-century still life hanging above the mantel. By contemporary British artist Brian Davies, the composition featuring Delft tiles, oysters, shrimp, and lemons is reminiscent of a Dutch still life. The Gates purchased the painting because it united elements of their house, which has Delft tile fire surrounds and lemon trees in the garden, with typical low country fruits-de-mer.

By far the grandest space in the house is the second-floor drawing room that has been described as "one of the most distinguished 18th century rooms in America." According to various fashions, the fine paneling in this room has been painted innumerable times and stripped twice. The Gates decided to keep the wood natural because they

loved the appearance of the warm golden grain. The room's mantel and overmantel are masterpieces of Georgian carving, made of several different types of wood chosen for their varying shades and textures and carved with shells, flowers, reeding, and a Greek key pattern. Charleston architectural historian Robert P. Stockton, in a history of the house, notes that all Georgian era woodwork may not have been painted, as previously assumed. In some cases, inferior wood was faux-grained to resemble more expensive woods, like the mahogany used in this mantelpiece. So the Gates decision to simply wax the room's wood may, in fact, be quite in keeping with the house's original style.

In decorating the room, the Gates deliberately strayed from Georgian taste, however, with the exception of a mid-eighteenth-century English chair upholstered in gray damask and softened with a tapestry pillow with a boar's-head pattern. Large contemporary sofas and armchairs upholstered in deep red are the room's primary furnishings. Matching red damask curtains hang from the tall windows, their hue enhancing the room's warm glow. Four prints from the elephant folio of nineteenth-century naturalist, John James Audubon, hang on the wall. These include a rendering of a flamingo, whose dark pink feathers and ochre and gray setting repeat the colors of the Heriz carpets covering the floor.

OPPOSITE: A small rear wing added to the house in the nineteenth century accommodates a diminutive library. Restoration architect Glenn Keyes designed Georgian-style paneling and moldings for the room, uniting it visually to the adjacent study.

Next to this large room is a smaller room that has been called both a withdrawing room and a card room throughout the centuries. Today, the Gateses often play cribbage and dominoes using antique game pieces and boards while sitting around an American Federal period game table before the fireplace. A Mouzon map of the Carolina colony, made around 1775, hangs on one wall and antique globes stand on the floor and cover several surfaces, reflecting one of Steve's collecting passions. The time-darkened orbs complement the room's waxed cypress walls, yet their appropriateness to the house is deeper than mere surface. These antique facsimiles of places far and near perfectly express the old-world cosmopolitanism of the house itself and the many generations of inhabitants who have enjoyed its worldly charms.

TOP LEFT: Fortuny silk in shades of deep apricot and platinum adds lustrous contrast to the study's waxed cypress paneling.

BOTTOM LEFT: The Gateses restored this room to its original proportions before installing contemporary kitchen accoutrements. The refrigerator stands in a niche that still contains a narrow servants' stair leading to the second floor.

OPPOSITE: A hunting scene by Gustav Zick hangs upon the carved cypress overmantel in the card room that opens off the large second-floor drawing room. Chippendale style chairs surround a reproduction pedestal table.

THE ISAAC MOTTE DART HOUSE
The Home of Dr. and Mrs. Eugene Gaillard Johnson, III

Charlestonians always have, and still do, love English style. The Isaac Motte Dart House, built circa 1806 by an attorney and cotton factor of that name, and restored by its present-day residents, Betsy and Gene Johnson, is a perfect illustration of this aesthetic penchant. In the late nineteenth century, fashionable English people and their Charleston counterparts began turning away from Georgian restraint and austerity. They embraced new, more highly decorated styles variously known as the Adamesque (after the Scottish architect Robert Adam), Regency (in honor of England's Prince Regent, George IV), and Federal (for the newly formed American government).

Delicate neoclassical detail; an eclectic borrowing from ancient Greek, Roman, Gothic, Egyptian, and Chinese sources; and a passion for applied details, whether in wallpaper, patterned fabric, or wood are all hallmarks of these styles. With the exception of Egyptian detail, all of the above can be found in the Isaac Motte Dart House, whose present-day owners have not only supervised a thorough renovation of the house, but also decorated with antiques and period reproductions representative of English Regency taste.

These furnishings complement the house's interior architectural detailing, which would be called Federal, rather than Regency, because it was manufactured, for the most part, in the United States during the post-Revolutionary period. At that time, Americans were consciously rejecting the Georgian

OPPOSITE:
The rear façade of Betsy and Gene Johnson's house is the result of a late-nineteenth-century addition. By re-creating the spacing of windows and doors found on the front façade, adding shutters copied from an original found on the property, and hiring a craftsman to create a gracefully curving stair rail, the new owners invoked the Federal-style balance and delicacy of the original structure.

ABOVE: The broad, center-hall plan of the Isaac Motte Dart House is reminiscent of Georgian architecture, but the tall portico with narrow columns lends Federal style grace to the façade.

style, which they associated with the colonial era. Despite the political rejection of England inherent in this shift, the Federal style still borrowed heavily from English aesthetics. To further clarify, the term Adamesque is often applied to the décor and architecture of the American Federal period and the British late Georgian and early Regency eras.

The Isaac Motte Dart House is built in a somewhat transitional style popular in Charleston at the turn of the eighteenth century which, in its massing, resembles a Georgian center hall house, but in decorative details, calls forth elements of Federal design. Rising one room deep and three stories high on a raised basement, the house originally boasted two large rooms opening off a central stair hall on its first and second floors. A small columned portico in the Federal style covers the front entrance to the house and a double-piazza (or two story porch) parallels the rear. A fanlight and sidelights surrounding the front door add more Federal-style detail to the exterior.

While the exterior details are somewhat restrained, glimpses of the dwelling's interior gained through the front door's sidelights indicate a far more lavish approach to decoration within. When present-day owners Betsy and Gene Johnson first peeked through these windows in 1993, they spied ornate plaster friezes with delicately wrought rosettes, acanthus leaf cornice moldings, and cypress wainscoting with carved chair rails. On their first tour of the house, the couple also discovered fine mantels ornamented with exquisite detail, including flowers, birds' nests, shells, garlands, and even a fox hunting scene.

At the time the Johnsons purchased it, the house was uninhabited and suffering from neglect, its plaster walls crumbling and its rear façade covered with tar paper. "It seemed just incredible to us that some-thing like this was just sitting here," recalls Betsy. Both descendents of old Charleston families, the Johnsons recognized the house as an architectural damsel in distress, and came to its rescue, bringing with them a collection of inherited furnishings, a passion for Regency style, and an expert restoration team. One of Charleston's foremost architectural restoration experts, Richard Marks, headed the team, which also included a veteran Charleston interior designer, James Evans, who had been involved in the decoration of the Johnsons' previous house.

One of the team's first priorities was cleaning and restoring the antique plaster and composition details that lend such grace and elegance to the rooms. Patty Hedock, a member of Marks' restoration team, carefully removed paint from the plaster and composition mantel decorations with gentle solvents and tiny tools, including dental picks. She recast missing elements from existing pieces and restored the ornamentation to its original, crisp design. A team of painters then applied paint in shades ranging from beige to pale apricot designed to highlight the three-dimensional nature of the decorative plaster friezes. The cypress wainscoting and chair rails, which are decorated with a guilloche pattern of interlocking circles in the drawing room and a triglyph pattern in the dining room, were painted in a glossy ivory to complement the matte texture of the plaster walls.

Architectural evidence and records indicated that the house, built for Isaac Motte Dart, was purchased and expanded in 1815 by Edward Washington

OPPOSITE: A center hall links the four rooms on the first floor of the house. The simple ornamentation of the painted cypress wainscoting and door surrounds is more reminiscent of Georgian than Federal design. A Chinese Buddha figure that belonged to Gene Johnson's grandmother sits upon an American table.

North. The addition of rooms on the back of the house transformed the single-pile residence into a double-pile, or two-room deep, dwelling. The addition was destroyed during 1989's Hurricane Hugo, but the Johnsons decided to build a new one, following the original footprint. Drawing inspiration from paneled rooms popular in late-eighteenth- and early-nineteenth-century Charleston, the Johnsons asked Marks to create a cypress-paneled library behind the drawing room. Marks designed a room lined with bookshelves featuring an overmantel decorated with a guilloche pattern modeled after the chair rail of the drawing room next door.

When he designed the cabinetry for the kitchen that forms the other half of the first floor addition, Marks also sought to visually unite it to the decoration of the existing rooms. In this case, he modeled the kitchen cabinets on the design of the wainscoting in the adjoining dining room. He also suggested placing a fanlight above the door connecting the two rooms, adding a note of elegance visible from either side.

While the major restoration and construction work was underway, the Johnsons lived in the 1823 Gothic Revival carriage house built at the rear of the property. This structure, now fully restored and nestled in an Italianate garden of boxwood and gravel walks that Gene designed, is operated today as the Wortham House Bed and Breakfast.

When they began decorating the main house, the new residents chose warm beige for the walls of the drawing and dining rooms, bringing color in with window treatments. In keeping with Regency style, they chose opulent damask fabric draped in toga-like folds over windows fitted with louvered

TOP LEFT AND OPPOSITE: Employing hundreds of colors applied with thousands of hand-carved wood blocks, Joseph Darfour's Monuments of Paris wallpaper depicts detailed scenes of early-nineteenth-century Paris.

TOP RIGHT: The Ramage & Ferguson mantel in the dining room combines aquatic, floral, and architectural motifs.

TOP LEFT: The garnishing of mantels was elevated to a high art in the Regency period. A pair of unmatched English armchairs flanks the mantel. Asian decorative objects, including a pair of antique vases and Ming-dynasty figures, are symmetrically placed, interspersed with portrait miniatures by unidentified American painters depicting Gene's ancestors.

BOTTOM LEFT: With its delicate lines, caning, and symmetrical design, this English Regency sofa is a classic example of the era's furniture. Typical Regency style upholstery includes a pair of round bolsters.

OPPOSITE: There are two focal points in the drawing room: a large portrait attributed to English Regency-era painter Sir Thomas Lawrence and a mantel with a fox hunting scene molded from composition and attributed to the Scottish firm of Ramage & Ferguson.

blinds. "If you want to have a house that looks like it really is a Charleston house, Jimmy Evans knows how to do it," says Mrs. Johnson, who hired the decorator to assist with fabric selection and other design decisions. "I think it's easy to overdo things, and overdoing is just not Charleston's style," she concludes.

After living in the house for several years, the Johnsons enriched the entertaining rooms' appearance, painting the walls of the drawing room a luminous hue of blue-green inspired by a color on the frame of an Italian mirror they owned. Their friend, fellow Charlestonian Price Cameron, suggested they make an even bolder Regency statement in the dining room by covering the walls with mural wallpaper popular in turn-of-the-eighteenth-century Europe and America. Specifically,

he suggested using *Les Monuments de Paris* design by Joseph Darfour, which was used by Washington at Mount Vernon and by Napoleon at Fontainebleau.

The richly colored, detailed scenic wallpaper complements the neoclassical decorative motifs of the Johnsons' dining room and adds the decorative ebullience that is associated with the Regency era. The final result in the dining room is a place where the eye does not so much rest as graze. The beautiful haut-relief of the plaster, with its processions of rosettes; the garlands, urns, and shells of the mantel; the blue and gray buildings of Paris, the swimmers in the Seine, and the shepherds upon its banks— these provide a feast for the eyes.

Betsy asserts that a monumental portrait ascribed to Sir Thomas Lawrence hanging in the drawing

ABOVE: The dining room's Monuments of Paris wall-paper is a hand-screened reproduction of a scenic panorama originally manufactured in 1814 by Joseph Darfour, re-created by The Twigs in cooperation with the Metropolitan Museum of Art. The plaster cornice molding is painted in several shades of beige and pale apricot to enhance the three-dimensional elements of the design.

OPPOSITE: Delicate neoclassical furniture, including a set of Hepplewhite chairs and a fine American sideboard, circa 1790–1810, share curvilinear lines that reflect the elegant draperies of blue brocade curtains. In keeping with traditional period window treatments, louvered blinds help control the flow of light and air.

room, adds ballast, balancing the visual weight of the dining room across the hall. According to the authors of *Style Traditions: Recreating Period Interiors* (Rizzoli: 1990), she made the perfect decision in acquiring this painting for the house. "When it comes to picture hanging, those who have dashing Regency ancestors painted by Sir Thomas Lawrence will have no problem in achieving the right effect[,]" state Stephen Calloway and Stephen Jones in their chapter describing Regency interiors.

This large portrait, acquired from Estate Antiques in Charleston, depicts an elegant woman of society clasping a muslin–clad daughter to her side. The mobile draperies of the subjects complement the sweeping, tasseled curtains of the room. The room's second focal point is a decorated mantel featuring a molded composition scene attributed to the Scottish workshop of Ramage & Ferguson. It depicts a pair of hounds chasing a fox in a highly detailed landscape. Garlands flank the scene, and

TOP LEFT: Neoclassical urns, garlands, and reeding decorate the ornate mantel in the Johnsons' drawing room, which is garnished with portrait miniatures painted on ivory and backed with plaits of woven hair.

BOTTOM LEFT: The palettes of the contemporaneous English Regency and American Federal styles tended toward bright, rich hues. In decorating their home, the Johnsons chose subdued interpretations of the deep reds, greens, and blues of the period.

OPPOSITE: Architectural restoration expert Richard Marks copied the guilloche pattern of interlocking circles on the library's overmantel from the drawing room's chair rail to create a sense of unity. Medieval tapestry-style upholstery on a pair of English armchairs and gout stool and a painting of a dog lend British flair to this cypress-paneled room. The backs of the cypress bookshelves are painted green to contrast with and visually recede from the rich amber tones of the unpainted paneling.

OPPOSITE: In the kitchen, an antique mantel and new cabinet doors with detailing inspired by the wainscoting of the adjacent dining room create a sense of age, as well as unity between the rooms. Marks recommended installing the Federal-style fanlight detail above the door connecting the two rooms to further this sense of continuity.

TOP LEFT Upstairs drawing room mantel: This exquisitely detailed scene from nature was molded from composition (a term referring to a mixture of glue and other materials), using a mold designed by the revered Scottish firm of Ramage & Ferguson. The importation of such ornamentation, popularized across the Atlantic by Robert Adam, was common among Charleston's well-to-do homeowners.

TOP RIGHT: The master bedroom, like the other rooms in the Johnsons' house, reveals an eclectic approach to décor found commonly in Charleston. The large, early-nineteenth-century American four-poster bed was purchased by Gene's grandmother at an auction in the mid-twentieth century. Although modern, the upholstered scroll-back chairs complement the shapes and scale of American Empire furniture of the early nineteenth century.

smaller garlands and reeding complete the decorative effect. Three other fine examples of Ramage & Ferguson composition work are found in the house, including an arrangement of birds and flowers in the upstairs drawing room and garland, shell, and urn motifs in the dining room.

An English Regency caned sofa, purchased from Charleston's Jack Patla Antiques and placed beneath the portrait, demonstrates the light, delicate approach to material and massing that characterizes Regency furniture. Symmetry was another hallmark of the style, expressed on the sofa with paired velvet bolsters. On the far wall, a pair of delicate Regency chairs sits beneath rococo gilt mirrors in perfect symmetry. A pair of Chinese vases, matching Ming-dynasty figures, and two portrait miniatures of Gene's ancestors garnish the mantel in a balanced arrangement that further reflects Regency era taste. "Density or clutter must be avoided and the symmetrical placing of paired things remains the best way in which the rational style of Regency rooms may be evoked," write the authors of *Style Traditions*.

A fascination with Gothic ornamentation and chinoiserie are two other aspects of Regency style that find expression in the Johnsons' house, particularly in the library. Heavy tapestry curtains and antique English furniture upholstered in matching tapestry

TOP RIGHT AND OPPOSITE: Quadrefoil windows on the second floor and lancet windows are typical elements of the Gothic style in which this carriage house was built in 1823. The Johnsons now operate it as the Wortham House Bed and Breakfast.

BOTTOM LEFT: Gene transformed the driveway into a European style allée flanked with boxwood and yew hedges and terminating in a brick folly. The folly's design was inspired by the Gothic style of the carriage house and other similar nineteenth-century Charleston dependencies.

lend a medieval feeling to this room. Imari china, Chinese foo dogs, and Korean chests inject an exotic Asian note, as does the blue and gold Chinese carpet, an early-twentieth-century import style that was popular in Charleston.

In the Johnsons' less formal rooms, the couple relaxed their dedication to Regency styles and principles. The kitchen, for example, was inspired by old-fashioned plantation kitchens. Having seen a moose head mounted above the kitchen mantel at Halidon Hill outside Charleston, Betsy insisted upon having the deer head similarly placed in her kitchen. Marks found an antique mantel with slightly distressed wood which lends a note of age to the kitchen, echoed by the rugged pine table Betsy chose for the room.

In the second and third floor rooms, the Johnsons combined their collections of inherited furniture, mostly American and English early-nineteenth-century pieces, with objects they have collected. The result is a comfortable eclecticism with a distinctly Charleston air. The master bedroom features a large, early-nineteenth-century mahogany four-poster bed. For draperies, Betsy selected plain, unbleached tea cloth. "In Charleston, everybody had tea cloth canopies on their four-poster beds," recalls the homeowner, who also chose the simple fabric to soften the light coming in through the room's tall windows.

While his wife focused on completing the interior decoration, Gene turned his energies and imagination to the landscape, designing, planting, and caring for an elaborate Italian-style formal garden. This choice of garden style is perfectly in keeping with the age of the house and its Regency décor. During the eighteenth and early nineteenth centuries, it was fashionable for well-to-do Americans and British to travel in Italy. When they returned,

they brought home a greater appreciation for the Roman roots of neoclassical design and a new interest in the principles of Italian garden design.

In particular, they adopted the concept of gardens arranged in geometrical spaces (or rooms) connected by axes defined by walkways and shrubberies.

Featuring boxwood parterres, gravel walks, towering Italian cypress, roses, crepe myrtle, and Carolina jasmine, the garden's geometric walkways and beds are filled with color and scent year-round. A stroll through the garden provides perfect vantage points from which to view the symmetrical beauty of the main house and the Gothic charm of the former carriage house. Larger garden rooms, such as the one directly behind the main house and in front of the carriage house, unfurl like beautiful tapestries before them. A long gravel allée, which also serves as a drive, links the garden rooms and leads to a tiny folly inspired by the brick Gothic-style dependencies popular in old Charleston. The end result is a seamless marriage of exterior and interior spaces that allows the mind and senses to travel back and linger in the gracious styles of turn-of-the-eighteenth-century Charleston.

OPPOSITE Wall ornament: A cast stone wall ornament inspired by an Italian garden sculpture depicting Bacchus nestles among the jasmine vines that climb the perimeter wall of the garden.

THE NATHANIEL RUSSELL HOUSE
A House Museum of Historic Charleston Foundation

Charleston's golden age of commerce reached its zenith at the turn of the eighteenth century, with Nathaniel Russell as one of its richest merchants. The second son of a wealthy Rhode Island family, Russell came to Charleston at the age of twenty-seven to make his fortune. Building a career by shipping rice, indigo, tobacco, and cotton, as well as slaves, to and from New England, the West Indies, South America, Virginia, Great Britain, continental Europe, West Africa, and Asia, he amassed a great fortune and gained entrée to Charleston's loftiest society. In 1808, he constructed a house in the high-style neoclassical mode which is both a lasting monument to his success and one of the city's architectural crown jewels.

As the site for his family's new home, Russell bought a large lot of land on Meeting Street, south of Broad Street, then and now one of the city's most fashionable addresses. He hired a builder whose name is lost to history to design a grand mansion in the Federal style, as the American interpretation of England's Adamesque style came to be known. Named after its best-known practitioner, Scottish architect Robert Adam, the style provided a decorative alternative to the stern dignity of the mid-to-late-eighteenth century's prevailing Georgian taste. Inspired by Greek and Roman motifs and architectural plans, Adam's architecture and interior design promoted balance and symmetry, inventive room shapes, elongated proportions, exuberant color, and lavish neoclassical ornamentation.

OPPOSITE: Wrought-iron balconies emblazoned with a cartouche of Nathaniel Russell's initials decorate the façade of this 1808 Federal style house that is one of Charleston's finest historic dwellings. Triple-sash windows open onto the balconies, offering views of the surrounding formal gardens and inviting ocean-borne breezes to cool the house.

ABOVE: A free-flying stair rises through the hall at the center of the house where portraits by Henry Benbridge (shown) and George Romney hang. The interior wall of the oval dining room echoes the stair's curve to create a dynamic space. Trompe l'oeil painting in shades of gray and white mimic plaster cornice moldings, and doors faux-grained to resemble mahogany add decorative detail. In contrast, the entrance hall, glimpsed through elaborately glazed and faux-grained doors, seems quite austere.

TOP LEFT: Chinese export porcelain in a double peacock and peony pattern adds color to the table while English silver and Irish and English crystal offer gleam. The epergne in the center of the table predates most of the room's furnishings, its complex rococo lines contrasting with the early nineteenth century's simpler silhouettes.

BOTTOM LEFT: A porcelain epergne made in Sevres, France is fashioned in the shape of the three muses, reflecting the period's obsession with classical Greek imagery. The wallpaper border of red and gold interlocking rings was created for the Nathaniel Russell House's twenty-first-century restoration, inspired by a geometric motif popular in the Federal period.

OPPOSITE: Charleston's furniture-making tradition reached its peak of excellence at the turn of the eighteenth century, yielding masterpieces such as this delicately inlaid mahogany sideboard, table, and Sheraton-style chairs. While neoclassical design was the primary influence upon the period's furniture, Gothic elements also appeared, as illustrated by the pointed arch pattern of the chair backs.

The tall, narrow façade of the Nathaniel Russell house distinguishes it from the typically broader, heavier edifices of its Georgian neighbors. Constructed of Carolina gray brick ornamented with imported white marble detail, the façade lifts lightly skyward from its garden setting. The façade is symmetrical, but a bay projects on the southeastern side of the house to accommodate a pair of oval entertaining rooms on the first and second floors. Typical of Adamesque design, these rooms lend dynamic tension to the house, where straight lines intersect curves and the principles of symmetry and asymmetry joust.

Visitors to the house enter from the street through a wrought-iron gate and formal garden that create a sense of ceremonial approach. In Nathaniel Russell's day, there were two types of visitors: Mr. Russell's business associates, who gathered in the square entrance hall at the front of the house and the small office Mr. Russell maintained just to the left of the front door, and social callers. The latter would move quickly through these plain rooms, ushered by servants through a pair of elaborately glazed and faux-grained doors into the heart of the house: a breathtaking central stair hall with golden walls and a free-flying spiral stair that winds toward the house's upper floors. Illuminated by a Palladian window, this delightfully asymmetrical hall is studded with doors faux-grained to resemble flame-grained mahogany; ebony, satinwood, and brass inlay; and even tortoiseshell. Trompe l'oeil painting resembling a plaster cornice and an elliptical plaster medallion add further ornamentation to the space.

OPPOSITE: A French chandelier and candelabra of gilded bronze were the only source of nocturnal illumination in this elegantly detailed oval drawing room that witnessed the Russell family's most formal entertainments. By candlelight, the room's walls and gilded moldings would have glowed with subtle beauty.

TOP LEFT: A pair of curved and mullioned mirrors adorns the interior wall of the oval drawing room, decorated with surrounds identical to the windows across the room. These served both functional and decorative purposes, reflecting light and creating symmetry.

TOP RIGHT: Several of the doors in the house were painted in a faux-bois style that imitated flame-grain mahogany, one of the period's most expensive and decorative woods. They have recently been restored to their original glory.

The decorative painting on the walls and doors were the work of nineteenth-century Charleston artisan, Samuel O'Hara, who directed potential clients to view his artisanship at "Mr. Russell's new building in Meeting Street . . . which he confidently believes has not been equaled by any in the city." At the turn of the twenty-first century, Historic Charleston Foundation, who maintains the building as a house museum, hired the finest contemporary artisans to re-create these decorative tours de force. On the first and second floors, the faux-grained doors open into entertaining rooms ornamented in lavish detail. These, too, have recently benefited from the extensive research and restoration project that has returned them to the polychrome glory of Nathaniel Russell's day.

Located on the first floor, the dining room's oval walls are covered with wallpaper tinted an intense turquoise shade called verditer, popularized by Robert Adam. This unpatterned paper hangs above cypress wainscoting painted white and is finished with a border print of interlocking rings, or guilloche, with highlights of gold and red that echo the warm tones of the room's fine wood furniture. This includes a mahogany dining table, sideboard, and chairs made in Charleston that display the delicate, tapering proportions favored during the Federal era. In addition to Charleston-made pieces, the Russells also owned furniture shipped from New York and England. Most of the silver, including the dramatic rococo-style epergne on the table, is English, reflecting the tendency of eighteenth- and early-nineteenth-century Charlestonians to patronize London's finest silversmiths. Chinese export porcelain graces the table, and a fine porcelain epergne made in Sevres, France that depicts the three graces in high neoclassical style stands on a demilune table against the far wall.

One turn up the cantilevered staircase leads to the second floor where the house's most highly decorated rooms are situated, above the hubbub and odors of the early-nineteenth-century streets. On this floor, a pair of curved double doors, faux-grained in imitation of mahogany on one side and faux-boule (or tortoise shell) on the other, opens into the drawing room. Mullioned mirrors on one

OPPOSITE: The drawing room captures and reflects the morning light with its gray walls, white wainscoting, and gilded cornice moldings. A pair of globes and English and European paintings hung salon style attest to Nathaniel Russell's international success as a merchant and the family's cosmopolitan tastes.

ABOVE: English tea accoutrements including a Worcester tea service, circa 1808, and a hot water urn made by late-eighteenth-century London silversmith, John Robbins, adorns a Charleston-made table. English Regency-style armchairs painted black with gilt decoration and neoclassical figures painted en grisaille descended through the Allston family, who lived in the house following the Russell family's residency.

end of the room balance identically mullioned windows across the oval space to create symmetry and reflect the light.

Apricot-colored wallpaper covers the plaster walls, and intricate cornice moldings gilded and painted in shades of oxblood, grisaille, and gold crown the room. Floral motifs and fretwork tinted with oxblood paint add more detail to the window surrounds rising like clusters of slender columns from faux-lapis-lazuli plinths. While such bold coloration might seem gaudy today, when such rooms were used primarily for evening entertainments and illuminated solely by candlelight, these bright hues and gleaming highlights glowed with subtle elegance.

The svelte curves of the drawing room's neoclassical furniture, including an American Récamier sofa, a French harp, and a music stand (probably English), reflect the period's taste for flowing Grecian lines. The present furnishings suggest the varied uses this chamber would have accommodated, including musical entertainments, dancing, games played on the mahogany card table, or sumptuous teas served on Old Paris porcelain. Tea was more frequently served, however, in the neighboring withdrawing room. This large room is situated at the front of the house, where it receives the greatest effects of sunlight and breezes that flow in through tall windows opening on three sides.

With soft gray walls, this room décor is more suited for daytime activities than that of the drawing room. Here, gilded, beaded cornice moldings, a gilded overmantel, and mirrors and paintings with gilt frames offer bright counterpoint to the muted wall color. The warm, red tones of highly polished mahogany furniture contrasts with black-painted furniture, including several armchairs and a fire screen, that was popular in the period. English and Italian art, as well as American portraits, hang on the walls, bespeaking the Russell family's status as wealthy, cultivated citizens of the world.

While fine English-made silver tea accoutrements betray a love of leisure and ostentatious social display, the room also witnessed meetings of the Russell ladies' philanthropic groups, including the Charleston Female Domestic Missionary Society, which ministered to poor and enslaved Africans, and the Ladies Benevolent Society. The remainder of the house, including a master bedchamber on the second floor, bedchambers on the third floor, and a family sitting room on the ground floor, are far less elaborately detailed. Although far from austere, these rooms were designed less to impress than to offer comfortable accommodations.

Three generations of the Russell family peopled these rooms before they passed out of their hands into those of an equally illustrious Charleston family, who added Victorian embellishments and furnishings without destroying the original Federal details. After the Civil War, the house became a school for young women, once again escaping significant redesign. As a result, the curators of Historic Charleston Foundation were presented the opportunity to restore the house to its original period style when they acquired it in 1974. Thanks to their diligence, the house now serves as a living-color legacy of the bold taste and brilliant lifestyle of Charleston's golden age.

OPPOSITE: Furniture painted black and illuminated with gilded or grisaille detail, such as this armchair made in England, circa 1800, was popular in England's Regency era and reflected the influence of lacquered furniture imported from China and Japan.

LEFT, TOP and BOTTOM: A dramatic scene from Shakespeare's Macbeth, painted by Charleston artist John Blake White in 1809, is among the oils hanging on the drawing room's walls. The architectonic window surrounds, with their tall, slender pilasters and overhanging entablatures, add three-dimensional detail to the walls, as does the multi-layered, gilded cornice molding.

OPPOSITE: Morning light illuminates the ornamental details of an Old Paris fruit cooler, an inlaid mahogany card table made in Charleston, circa 1810, and an American giltwood oval mirror.

FROM FEDERAL
TO GREEK REVIVAL

THE WILLIAM AIKEN HOUSE
A Historic Property of Patrick Properties

Like their friends and family back in mother England, the wealthy residents of eighteenth- and nineteenth-century Charleston were extremely status conscious. The ways they measured social and financial success were myriad, from the silver on their tables to the equipage in their carriage houses. When it came to affluent Charlestonians' homes, the list of necessary attributes was long and expensive. Among these was a commodious dwelling at a fashionable address that efficiently captured cool coastal breezes; rooms decorated in au courant style; and an art collection combining works by European Old Masters and English and American portrait artists.

"It was true that anyone with enough money could assemble such collections," writes Maurie McInnis in *In Pursuit of Refinement: Charlestonians Abroad 1740 to 1860*, the catalogue for a 1999 Gibbes Museum of Art exhibition of the same title. "[B]ut the key was in knowing what to collect—and that is how one communicated one's refinement," the author concludes.

Although the William Aiken House, at the corner of King and Ann Streets, passed out of private hands barely fifty years after it was constructed (becoming the headquarters for the Southern Railway for more than a century), it still miraculously communicates the refinement of the illustrious Charleston families that inhabited it. Thanks for this are due not only to the timeless elegance of the dwelling, built in the first half of the nineteenth

OPPOSITE: In the 1830s, Governor William Aiken added an octagonal wing to the house, nearly doubling its size with a pair of grand entertaining rooms decorated in the Greek revival style then popular. The original piazza was extended to wrap around this wing.

ABOVE: The entrance to the William Aiken House is typical of the Federal style Charleston single house. A fanlight with sinuous mullions surmounts the paneled door that opens onto a marble-floored piazza. Like a Greek or Roman colonnade, this porch features Doric columns supporting a ceiling decorated with dentils and other classical motifs.

century, but also to the refinement and skills of the late-twentieth-century preservationists and design professionals who restored and refurnished it in period style.

The National Trust for Historic Preservation has maintained regional offices in the building since 1977, but actual refurbishment of the property did not begin until it was purchased by Patrick Properties, a private real estate development group which owns several historic buildings on King Street. Company founders Celeste and Michael Patrick selected Glenn Keyes, one of Charleston's most highly reputed conservation architects, to oversee the eighteen-month restoration project. While directing the cleaning, repair, and replacement of damaged and missing architectural elements, Keyes also collaborated with interior designer Paula Adams, who selected paint colors, floor coverings, upholstery, and draperies for the house. Antiques expert Vangie Rainsford collected furniture, decorative objects, and artwork that complete the house's conjuring act, re-creating the elegance of Charleston's golden age.

The end result, a resplendent urban estate now used for private events (as well as the regional National Trust office), recaptures the styles of three distinct design movements that swept early-nineteenth-century Charleston. These include the Federal style, in which James Mackie built the original three-story single house in 1807, before selling it to William Aiken, a prominent merchant and railroad entrepreneur. This classic Charleston-style dwelling features a typical Federal entrance, with a fanlight above a door flanked by Doric pilasters. Within, the rooms display the ornamentation favored in the period, including wood and plaster moldings meticulously fashioned in neoclassical motifs.

A carriage house at the end of the property, built in 1810, expresses the Gothic revival style, an aesthetic reminiscent of the architecture of feudal England that was popular in Charleston for utilitarian outbuildings. When William Aiken, Sr. died in a carriage accident in the 1830s, his son Governor William Aiken Jr. inherited the estate and further embellished it. He is credited with adding a polygonal wing that doubled the size of the house to accommodate two large entertaining rooms decorated in the Greek Revival style that was gaining popularity in the American South at that time.

The original structure conforms to the single-house plan favored by Charlestonians: a single-pile (one room deep) center-hall residence that turns a narrow façade to face the street. A double piazza graces the long southeastern façade, shading the interior from the strong semi-tropical sun and creating a partially enclosed living space facing a private garden. A three-story staircase rises through the center of the house, illuminated and ventilated with windows opening on either side. Elaborate plaster moldings decorate the ceilings of each landing, with a gilded eagle spanning the third floor ceiling, a favorite Federal motif signaling post-Revolutionary patriotism.

OPPOSITE: Resplendent in aqua and gold, the first floor ballroom is naturally cooled by glazed French windows that open onto three sides of the long room. Continental European art and antiques reflect the cosmopolitan tastes of early-nineteenth-century Charlestonians. The room's simple yet massive cornice moldings and gilded window cornices typify the early expression of the Greek revival style.

TOP LEFT: The drawing room's mantel was removed from the house by the president of the Southern Railway in the 1920s. During the recent restoration project, Patrick Properties retrieved it from a barn in Virginia and commissioned the repair of its intricate composition details, which include reeding, urns, garlands and other popular Federal motifs.

TOP RIGHT: This plaster medallion graces the formal drawing room of the William Aiken House. Fashioned in the Federal style, its details include a corona of anthemia leaves encircled by rosettes. Many of these rosettes and leaves are replacement pieces, made in plaster from molds taken from the original medallion.

OPPOSITE: The lyrical neoclassical garlands, frets, and foliation of the formal drawing room demonstrate the influence of Regency England's premier architect, Robert Adam, upon American tastes during the Federal period. The custom-made carpet evokes the Adamesque style as well, employing motifs from the design notebooks of the Adam brothers.

TOP LEFT AND OPPOSITE: Interior designer Paula Adams recreated Federal period window treatments with swags of tasseled Scalamandré silk. A 1920s reproduction of a Federal style mantel, decorated with an elliptical shield in its center, and a pair of Regency style armchairs, painted black, are also appropriate to the period of this part of the house.

BOTTOM LEFT: The original single-house portion of the William Aiken House included an elegant central stair hall. The landings on each floor feature French doors surmounted by arched windows and intricately plastered ceilings. The small gilded bronze chandelier is made in a style favored by Federal era Charlestonians, who often purchased such lighting fixtures during trips to France.

The room opening to the left of the entrance hall, now decorated as a gentleman's study, represents a triumph of historic restoration. The original wooden moldings were removed in the 1920s by the Southern Railway Company and installed in their Washington, D.C. headquarters. Glenn Keyes took careful measurements of these moldings and re-created them with the help of a team of artisans, returning this room to its original Federal appearance. A similarly proportioned room decorated with plaster moldings stands across the center hall. Now used as the first floor dining room, this space is dwarfed by the large ballroom next door, where fulsome Greek Revival decorations make the dining room's Federal details seem almost fragile by comparison.

This octagonal ballroom, filling the ground floor of the 1830s addition to the house, reflects the new tastes of mid-nineteenth-century Charlestonians, who enthusiastically embraced the bold Greek Revival style. While still rooted in classical architecture and design, this new aesthetic favored more robust shapes and gestures over the Federal era's delicate garlands and depictions of mythological figures. The room's cornice moldings, drawn from the decoration of Greek and Roman temple entablature, and the plump plaster leaves of the ceiling medallion are typical of the Greek Revival's vocabulary and massing.

Interior designer Paula Adams drew inspiration from period rooms when she selected a palette of aqua and gold for the room and designed ornately

draped and tasseled curtains using Scalamandré re-production fabric. These hang from gilded cornice boards that were popular in the Greek Revival period, becoming more and more highly orna-mented as the style evolved. Furnishings that are heavier and more ornate than their Federal period predecessors gleam with gilt as well. A French gilded bronze chandelier, circa 1827, provides il-lumination, sparking highlights upon gilded Louis Quinze-style chairs and an Italian marble-topped table with gilded legs.

These furnishings reflect the tendency of the Charlestonians of this era to shop abroad, par-ticularly for lighting fixtures and artwork like the marble statue of Minerva, the Roman goddess of wisdom, that stands in one corner of the room. Although this statue was carved in Philadelphia, a nineteenth-century copy of a classical prototype, it is typical of the sculpture Charlestonians favored at the time, often shipping items back from Italy after enjoying a Grand Tour. The ballroom's continental furniture complements this room's large scale and formal appearance.

A trip to the floor above repeats this lesson in the evolution of domestic style in Charleston. The second floor landing of the original 1807 structure is embellished in pure Federal style, with precise, lace-like plaster ceiling embellishments and a small *bronze-d'oré* chandelier. The cornice moldings and mantel of the formal drawing room reflect the same neoclassical delicacy, which is repeated below in a new rug, custom made using decorative motifs from the sketchbooks of the Adam broth-ers, the Scots-born progenitors of Federal tastes. While the gilt furnishings currently used in the room are slightly heavier in appearance than the more attenuated pieces favored in the period, their combined sturdiness and opulence better suit the house's current use as an event venue.

The tapering legs of the dining table in the second floor dining room more closely represent the style of furnishings that would have graced this house in the early nineteenth century, as does the triple mirror above the mantel, made in England in the Regency style. Regency chairs, painted black and stenciled, stand beneath the four tall windows that balance each other in perfect symmetry across the rectangular room. Glazed French doors open from this room into the brilliant salmon-colored ballroom next door. Here, as below, the octagonal room's weightier furnishings, plaster moldings, and window treatments reiterate how Greek Revival tastes contrasted with those of the Federal era.

In the days of Governor Aiken's residency, this room would have witnessed many grand entertain-ments and family gatherings. Today, weddings are frequently celebrated in the second floor ballroom, where a fine copy of a Guerard portrait of Cupid and Psyche hangs upon the wall in celebration of romance. Diligence in historic research and excel-lence of craftsmanship are the foundations of the restoration of this grand mansion. But romance lies at the heart of the project—a love affair with Charleston's past and the cosmopolitan elegance that defined it.

OPPOSITE AND NEXT TWO PAGES: The glowing red walls, reminiscent of Pompeii, and pale blue ceiling of the second floor ballroom are selected to make the most of candlelight and create an enchanting space for evening entertainments. Gilded details include window cornices and a pair of caryatids that support the reproduction Empire-style table in the center of the room.

SOUTHERN COLLECTIVE UNCONSCIOUS

JOHNSON'S WESTERNMOST TENEMENT
The Home of Kathleen Rivers

Interior designer Kathleen Rivers' upbringing had the perfect ingredients for the acquisition of classic southern style. "My mother loved English decorating and my father was a very serious collector of Chinese porcelain," the Atlanta native says. "My father also loved to bird hunt, so as a young child, I would go out with him to stay in these simple country places. With my mother I would tour the countryside in search of tucked away antique shops." Kathleen also credits the Italian villas and French country houses she visited during early travels for inspiring her sense of taste. Cataloging these varied and far-flung influences, she sums up by paraphrasing Oscar Wilde: "The eye sees, but the mind brings with it the means to see."

"If I bring a style of eclecticism to my work, it is a compilation of all the things I have been exposed to," she explains. "People who have had a broad and diverse background, or who have travel experience, tend to accumulate the things they see and embrace them in their lives." Throughout her adult life, Kathleen has been acquiring a collection of furniture, decorative objects, and artworks that includes Chinese and English porcelains; American, French, English, and Italian furniture; and antique and contemporary paintings from Europe and America. Three years ago, she bought a house in downtown Charleston that provided the perfect setting for her cherished possessions.

"The moment I walked into this house, I felt that it evoked something very powerful in my southern

OPPOSITE AND ABOVE: Kathleen Rivers' house is the westernmost of a group of four row houses built circa 1801–1803 by William Johnson and known as Johnson's Row. Its second owner added embellishments to the simple Adamesque façade, including the wrought-iron balcony and stucco quoins on the corners.

upbringing," she recalls. "When I saw the rich patina on the enormous plank floors, which just by their size alone declared they were from a very old period, I fell in love with the house." Wooden walls, creaky steps, and doors that hung slightly askew all reminded her of antique southern houses. "Then to walk upstairs, and feel the light pouring in from the southeastern exposure of the house, and to see the beautiful mantels, the old glass in the windows, the tall ceilings—all this just spoke Charleston to me." And yet, something about the house also reminded her of Europe, especially Paris, where three- and four-story townhouses line narrow streets, their windows framing views of irregular rooflines not unlike those that Kathleen can see from her upper windows. "The first floor made me think of the low country; the second floor, of Europe; and the third floor, of the American South," says Kathleen, who bought the house and moved her possessions in within weeks of first seeing it.

The row house is one of four adjacent structures built between 1801 and 1803 as rental properties by William Johnson. Designed in the Adamesque style, the house is a modestly proportioned center-hall structure, with two rooms opening off a central stair hall that ascends through three floors to a fourth-story attic. All four structures are built of stucco-faced brick, but this, the most western of the row houses, is further embellished with a graceful wrought-iron balcony and stucco quoins that add an air of elegance to the façade. These details, speculates architectural historian Robert Stockton in a history of the house, date from the first decade of the nineteenth century, when the house was purchased by Captain James Tate. As a resident-owner (as opposed to a tenant), he added embellishments that were not shared by the contiguous rental properties. After Tate's family sold the house in 1843, it reverted to rental status, housing a wide

variety of tenants, including a French tinsmith, an American antiques dealer, and an Italian grocer. Several of the tenants operated businesses out of the ground floor rooms. In the late nineteenth century, a wooden structure connecting the main house to a two-story kitchen house behind it was built, and in the 1930s, two-thirds of the ground-floor, street-front room was transformed into a garage. Kathleen's decoration of the house connects all these parts of the house and the strands of its history in subtle ways. For example, she decided to transform the small front room on the first floor into a home office. "This was a way for me to embrace the idea that this had been the commercial part of the house," she explains.

The designer upholstered the walls of the small room, which had most recently been used as a laundry room, with chocolate-brown burlap and furnished it with an eighteenth-century French desk and an early-nineteenth-century English linen press—both elegant, yet utilitarian pieces. She designed a wall of dark wood paneling that complemented the furniture's finish to screen a powder room serving the ground floor. Not wanting to block the flow of light from the front of the house into her office and the stair hall beyond, she included three clerestory windows that bring soft, indirect illumination into the space.

OPPOSITE: A courtyard paved with stone and brick parallels the house, leading to a door on the side that opens into a central stair hall. A gate leads to a larger courtyard at the rear of the property overlooked by the kitchen dependency. A mix of evergreens and flowering trees provides year-round shade, scent, and color.

TOP LEFT: Paneling painted shades of cream and ochre create a stately atmosphere in the dining room, decorated with American and English furniture and artwork dating from the period of the house's construction. A Thomas Sully portrait of an actor glows warmly in the light of a lamp placed atop a butler's desk attributed to Duncan Phyfe. Glossy leaves from trees in the garden are arranged in an Edgefield-style glazed pitcher.

TOP RIGHT: A French country table, Italian chairs, and modern brass-and-marble tables contribute to making this kitchen dining- and sitting-area the most eclectic and casual of the house's rooms. Although the space is small, the use of a large landscape painting and a glass door overlooking the garden makes it seem more expansive. The choice of round furniture creates a sense of flow and prevents the room from feeling awkward or cramped.

OPPOSITE: The original wood door, fine early-nineteenth-century English linen press, and paneled-wood wall, combined with walls covered with dark brown burlap, create the impression of a wood-paneled room in this small office space. A rustic iron chandelier and a stone floor add more notes of natural color and texture to the cozy room.

While soft light from these windows flows into the right side of the entrance hall, much brighter light floods in from the dining room on the other side. This room's white and ochre paneling glows throughout the day, thanks to tall windows in two walls that frame views of the house's courtyard garden. "A friend of mine suggested that I make this room look not so much like a dining room as a welcoming hall, since my main drawing room is upstairs," Kathleen explains. To achieve this appearance, Kathleen selected a round table of the style and size that might be found in an English entrance hall. She placed a velvet-clad camelback sofa against one wall, and arranged upholstered dining chairs around the periphery of the room.

Most of the furniture and artwork in this room corresponds with the date of the house's construction, including a very fine butler's desk of inlaid mahogany, made circa 1810, attributed to Duncan Phyfe. Above this which hangs a portrait by Thomas Sully. Raised in Charleston and popular as a portrait painter among well-to-do Charlestonians, Sully painted this portrait of actor George Cooke in 1811. Kathleen discovered the painting at the Charleston International Antiques Show in 2005 and could not resist bringing it home for approval. "It's been hanging there ever since," she adds.

A wooden addition originally designed to accommodate modern plumbing facilities connects the main house and its brick dependency, which was built as a kitchen but later transformed into living quarters. Late-nineteenth-century owners returned the brick dependency to its original use and transformed the connecting structure into a passageway. Kathleen uses it as a bar, placing an English sideboard along one wall where a monumental oil portrait of a late-eighteenth-century French lady hangs. Mounted antlers and a collection of feathers add a country touch to this narrow room, while

Italian chairs upholstered with animal print fabric add a note of whimsical eclecticism. "I like to use leopard or other animal prints because they add liveliness to a room," notes Kathleen.

This same playful approach to eclecticism permeates the kitchen dining area, which functions as a multipurpose space. "I wanted it to be a comfortable place to sit and watch television, or have a romantic dinner, or entertain grandchildren, or have girlfriends over for tea," she explains. Two petite armchairs provide cozy seating around a French country table, and a pair of contemporary brass and marble tables serve as stylish occasional tables for cups of tea or cocktails. A modern hanging lamp with a parchment shade injects another contemporary note to the room and repeats the round shapes of the tables and the chairs. "I am a feng shui advocate, and I chose all those round shapes to help make that very square, angular space feel softer," says the designer.

Kathleen chose a large landscape by artist Frank Strazzulla to hang on the wall to create a sense of expansiveness in the small room. "That painting makes me think of endless possibilities," she says. But she also enjoys looking out the plate glass door that opens into the garden beyond. Paved with stone and old brick, the garden was recently redesigned by Charleston-based landscape architect Sheila Wertimer, who reshaped its brick pathways and refined and updated its selection of plants.

OPPOSITE: "This is the most popular room in the house," says Kathleen of the passageway between the kitchen and the dining room where guests can pour themselves a glass of wine or prepare a cocktail-hour libation. An eighteenth-century French aristocrat painted in oil on panel looks on from above the room's English sideboard.

LEFT: Pillows upholstered in Italian fabric sit on a fine French sofa, circa 1810. Chinese porcelain, Japanese prints, an Oushak carpet, and Adamesque architectural details add a further medley of styles to the room, but white muslin upholstery and the room's cool green and white palette unify the various styles into a sophisticated whole.

OPPOSITE: Morning sun fills the drawing room with light, pouring in through two windows and a gib door that opens onto a balcony placed on the southeastern façade of the building. Breezes also flow in through the windows, which face the direction of the harbor where the Ashley and Cooper Rivers join the Atlantic Ocean. A large charcoal drawing by Charleston-based artist Douglas Balentine adds a contemporary touch to the room's décor.

A mix of glossy-leafed evergreens, including camellias, tea olive, fatsia, ligustrum, boxwood, loquat, and yew create a year-round bower of verdant shade with seasonal bursts of color and scent.

"Welcome to Paris," Kathleen says to first-time guests when they climb the stairs and enter her second floor drawing room. "There is nothing in here particularly priceless, but the simplicity of the muslin upholstery combined with the few fine antiques gives this room a classically, yet understated, refined aura," she adds, describing what feels to her so Parisian about the space.

Certainly the room's celadon and cream palette, its intimate yet elegant proportions, and the graceful curves of its furnishings are reminiscent of a sophisticated urban French salon. A fine French sofa, circa 1810, sets the tone. Upholstered in white muslin,

it is complemented by two French armchairs, also covered in white muslin, and a mid-nineteenth-century round table Kathleen purchased from French antique dealers. Blue and white Canton china collected by her parents, a pair of Japanese screens, and an antique Oushak carpet invoke the exotic, calling to mind the French penchants for chinoiserie, japonisme, and orientalism. Yet the delicate neoclassical ornamentation of the mantel and the gilded mirror above it speak of English and American early-nineteenth-century style, reminding visitors that they are in Charleston, not Paris.

Although the spacious guest room above this room expresses the same geographic range of style, Kathleen describes it as being most reminiscent of the American South. "It's not overdone, and it feels feminine without being too fancy or having too much in it," she says. In classic southern style, Kathleen decorated with heirlooms, including an English piecrust tilt-top table inherited from her mother and a landscape painting above the mantel. But her love of French style comes through in the red-and-white toile used to upholster the

TOP LEFT: Exquisitely detailed composition ornaments the drawing room mantel, including the garlands, urns, egg-and-dart moldings, and classical figures that were favored in England's Adamesque and America's Federal styles. Kathleen's collection of silver compacts, boxes, cigarette cases, and cups reveal the craftsmanship of nineteenth- and early-twentieth-century English and American silversmiths.

BOTTOM LEFT: Late-nineteenth-century hand-painted tiles with naturalistic depictions of flowers and birds contrast with the stylized neoclassical details of the parlor's mantel.

OPPOSITE: The third floor rooms have much less ornate moldings than the house's first two floors, creating a slightly less formal air. Kathleen used red-and-white toile fabric to upholster furniture and drape the windows of this room, creating a serenely unified palette befitting a bedroom.

furniture and drape the windows. Once the toile curtains were hung beneath matching padded valences, Kathleen realized that the red in the fabric matched the color of the painted and tiled rooftops framed by the windows. The lavatory placed against the wall of the room and skirted with toile is another European touch, inspired by old country hotels she visited in France.

In a kind of conjuring act, Kathleen seems to have evoked a little bit of every generation and nationality that has lived in this historic townhouse. Her décor exhibits both English restraint and a country French approach to mixing pieces from various periods and styles with ease. While the drawing room is suggestive of Parisian sophistication, her dining room is reminiscent of the handsome comfort of English and Southern country estates. While there is a touch of Italian modishness in the kitchen dining area, with its bright orange chairs and marble-topped metal tables, the mood in the garden is pure Charleston, with the sweetly spicy scent of tea olives, the mossy bricks, and the sound of nearby church bells. "What I love about this house is that is doesn't feel trumped up to be anything other than what it is," says Kathleen. "It is an authentic example of what Charleston is about, which is an indescribable nostalgia for certain things and places that are a part of our collective experience."

ANGLO-COLONIAL STYLE

THE INGLIS ARCH HOUSE
A Private Residence

A collection of masonry dwellings, now known as Rainbow Row, stands shoulder-to-shoulder on East Bay Street, where their original merchant residents once lived and worked near the wharves serving Charleston's international trade. Today, this trade has moved farther up the Cooper River, and over the centuries, these homes, which once accommodated offices and shops in their ground floors, have become some of Charleston's most sought-after residential real estate. Like much of downtown Charleston, however, they suffered the depredations of time, semitropical weather, and post–Civil War economic depression in the late nineteenth and early twentieth centuries.

Their transformation from dilapidated tenements to charming residences began with the vision of Dorothy Porcher Legge, a decorator and preservationist who lived in one of the townhouses in the 1930s. In an effort to draw attention to the charms of the block of old buildings, she conceived a scheme to have them painted in pastel shades associated with Colonial Caribbean architecture. The name Rainbow Row was bestowed upon the block which is now one of Charleston's signature architectural destinations.

In addition to their collective history, each townhouse has its own small piece of history to contribute. This is certainly true of the Inglis Arch House, built in 1778, destroyed soon after by fire, and rebuilt in 1782. The house is named for its original builder, George Inglis, but its second inhabitants, the mercantile firm of Leger and Greenwood, are

OPPOSITE: The Inglis Arch House is one of several tall, masonry townhouses that form the block known as Rainbow Row. While presenting rather severe facades along East Bay Street, many of these houses have spacious gardens behind that offer quiet escape from the bustling city traffic.

ABOVE: An iron gate leads into the paved forecourt of the eighteenth-century dependency now associated with the Inglis Arch House. The original two-story structure, once a kitchen house, is visible above the one-story walls of a twentieth-century addition that now houses a library and hallway.

better known to history as importers of the tea that was seized by Charleston patriots in the Charleston Tea Party of 1775. When the present resident of the Inglis Arch House excavated the garden behind it in preparation for installing a swimming pool, her restoration contractor, Richard Marks, discovered an unspent Revolutionary-era musket ball in the ground. Standing close to the harbor, the houses of Rainbow Row were damaged by warfare in both the American Revolution and the long siege of Charleston during the Civil War.

At some point in its history, the house attained Greek Revival details upon its façade, including a parapet roofline, which was replaced in the twentieth century with a triangular pediment more in keeping with the Federal style that would have prevailed at the time it was built. Although this façade rises directly from the sidewalks of busy East Bay Street, it offers easy access to quiet interior spaces and gardens through an arched opening at ground level. This arch leads into a quaint brick-lined alley with openings to houses on both sides and an iron gate through which lawns, hedges, and garden paths can be seen.

From this gate, glimpses can also be seen of a brick outbuilding with pale salmon-colored stucco walls punctuated by two black iron medallions—the ends of earthquake bolts used to restore the structure after the earthquake of 1886. Architectural evidence suggests that this building, once the kitchen house of a neighboring property, dates from the mid-eighteenth century. Today, it is a dependency of the Inglis Arch House, and is surrounded by pleasure gardens on three sides.

"We bought the house because its first floor rooms are actually at ground level, so you can walk right out into the garden and have wonderful garden views from almost every room in the house," says one of the owners. "We didn't want two houses,

but that is what we ended up with." Unlike many other Charlestonians, whose main houses often come with one or two unattached dependencies, the present owners decided not to attach the outbuilding to the main house or to transform it into guest quarters. Instead, they envisioned it as an adjunct to their home—a separate building devoted to work and play, with a library, two home-offices, and informal entertaining areas.

They retained Marks as their restoration contractor, working with him to remodel the dependency, which had been enlarged in the 1940s, to fulfill these functions. "The addition to the kitchen house was almost completely bricked in," recalls one of the homeowners, who wanted to open it up to the gardens that surround it. The result is a long room with a vaulted ceiling supported by massive, hand-hewn trusses and tall windows and French doors that address the gardens. Lined with bookshelves and furnished with Edwardian sofas and chairs, it recalls the mood of the great halls of England's oldest country estates.

The residents hired Charleston-based interior designer Amelia Handegan to help them pull together furniture and decorative objects brought from previous homes in Washington, New York, and Palm Beach. "Amelia has a deserved reputation for being good with color," says one of the residents, who worked collaboratively with Handegan to integrate a free-wheeling collection of English, Moroccan, Irish, Balinese, and Indian objects into the two

OPPOSITE: Added in the twentieth century and remodeled in the twenty-first century, this hallway connects the large library to the original two-story dependency that has served as kitchen, carriage house, and slave quarters over the centuries. Nineteenth-century English bamboo consoles line one wall, facing windows that open onto the paved forecourt.

dwellings. The end result is an Orientalist-infused eclecticism reminiscent of late-nineteenth-century English style when fashionable Britons decorated their homes with exotic souvenirs from their country's far-flung colonies.

This highly charged eclecticism is a style that has long appealed to the homeowners, who enjoyed travels to Bali, Morocco, and India. While souvenirs of these travels found their way into a former Palm Beach Key West-style residence, the homeowners' previous apartments in Washington and New York tended more towards Edwardian English style. In addition to purchasing fine English antiques for these homes, such as a dozen signed Windsor chairs, they also commissioned Edwardian-style upholstered pieces designed by David Eastman.

These comfortable sofas and lounge chairs, covered with tufted burgundy velvet, form seating areas beneath the giant trusses of the vaulted ceiling of the library. While a few Asian elements infuse this room, including a Korean Buddha figure, a Korean coffee table, and a contemporary Chinese

painting by Yang Yanping, the overall atmosphere is reminiscent of country English style. A large antique English worktable stands at one end of the room, surrounded by the Windsor chairs, providing a perfect place to peruse the many reference books that line the room's wooden shelves. Several sheep—witty decorative objects designed by the herd by Francois and Claude Lalanne—are placed so they look out the French doors toward the rear garden, lending a distinctly bucolic air to the room.

A hallway connects the library to the original dependency structure. With a wall of windows framing views of the garden, this hallway opens into another large room that was once used as a carriage house. With English bamboo console tables flanking one wall, this hallway continues the theme of British Colonial Orientalism that finds even fuller expression in the living- and dining-room area. With its curtained walls, patterned floor, and tall windows, this room feels almost like a tented garden pavilion. "I wanted some whimsy in that room," notes one of the residents. "This part of the house is almost like a playhouse in the summer

TOP LEFT: The residents suggested using this Korean table to hold the powder room's water basin. Designer Amelia Handegan found the copper vessel, Asian-inspired wallpaper, and gilded sconces.

BOTTOM LEFT: A Balinese wedding headboard provides an exotic focal point in the sitting area. Seating is provided by a Balinese daybed, antique bamboo chairs, and a bamboo and rattan lounge chair of Indonesian design. A mother-of-pearl inlaid table from India adds yet another exotic note to this whimsical sitting area.

OPPOSITE: Large arched doorways were transformed into windows and Asian-inspired fabric hung tent-like along the walls and windows to create a pavilion atmosphere in this long room. One end is devoted to dining, with an English pedestal table paired with bamboo chairs.

when the doors are all opened and we go in and out to the garden and the pool."

Handegan found the silk damask with a subtle arabesque pattern of red on a pale apricot field that lavishly covers all the walls of the room. She also recommended hiring Charleston-based decorative painter Kristen Bunting to decorate the floor, covering its hardwood boards with an Orientalist motif. When the ceiling was removed to reveal original support beams, Handegan suggested covering the raw surfaces of the wood between the beams with bamboo cloth, adding yet another Asian element.

The residents worked with Handegan to create a living and dining area in this tent-like space using some of their favorite exotic finds, including a

carved and painted Balinese wedding headboard, a Balinese daybed, and an Indian table with inlaid mother-of-pearl. "I've always collected those tables, because I like using them with English antiques," one of the homeowners explains. "They lighten up the atmosphere in what my husband calls 'a room full of brown furniture.'"

To balance these highly charged Asian pieces, a few pieces of "brown furniture" are scattered about the room, including a fine antique English pedestal table and a rare Irish mirror over the mantel. Four bamboo chairs reminiscent of British colonial décor in India provide seating. "I love that Amelia upholstered them in that shocking orange velvet," says one of the residents. "One of my favorite pieces in that room is the bamboo and rattan

LEFT: Charleston decorative painter Kristen Bunting covered the floors of the old kitchen house with a pattern drawn from Asian textiles. An antique brass-embossed chest, possibly from Morocco, adds more texture and pattern to the room.

OPPOSITE: Rosy amber colored marble covers the countertop in the kitchen where JMO Woodworks created butler's pantry-style cabinets. Floor stenciling and floor-to-ceiling draperies create a sense of visual unity between this space and the living-dining room next door.

lounge chair and ottoman, which I think of as a kind of meditation chair."

Decorative motifs from the living area continue into the kitchen, where the same red-and-white stenciling covers the floor and patterned curtains drape the large windows. Here, the carpenters of JMO Woodworks, who also designed the bookcases in the library, created butler's pantry-style cabinetry. Handegan found the amber-colored, polished marble for the kitchen counter and the large baker's rack that holds a collection of pots, platters, and Asian decorative objects. This kitchen serves as a summer kitchen for pool- and garden-related entertainments, as well as for the guests who occasionally stay in the dependency. But rather than devote the upstairs rooms to bedrooms, the residents turned them into offices, with tables, desks, and computer equipment, with only a small sleeping area.

Just as the original owners of this East Bay townhouse once combined business with leisure, so the present-day owners enjoy working and living in this eighteenth-century compound. One reason they chose this property out of the many they considered was its informal architecture, indicative of the mixed use its buildings had enjoyed over the years. "Charleston is an amazing city, where people still have ballrooms in their houses," one of the residents comments. "But if we had bought one of those formal houses with museum-quality moldings around the rooms, we would have had to be more circumspect. The advantage of this property is that we can express a little more personality and whimsy." And while the final effect is indeed fanciful, its Anglo-Orientalist style is rooted in the fact of Charleston's international trade, including the importation of oriental tea leaves that helped spark the conflict between the royal colony of Carolina and its mother country.

A GREEK REVIVAL SINGLE HOUSE
The Home of Merrill Benfield

OPPOSITE: The austere hand-planed cypress façade of Merrill Benfield's Greek Revival single house offers little hint of the freewheeling eclecticism and inventive design that takes place behind its mullioned windows. However, the glimpse of two marble busts, visible through the ground floor windows, suggests that a collector lives here.

ABOVE: Ancient Chinese vases and a Greek Revival lantern decorate the entrance hall. From this space, Merrill's elegant home office, ingeniously tucked into the drawing room, can be seen to advantage. A fine Chippendale chair offers seating at the antique English desk and an eighteenth-century Russian clock marks the hours as they pass.

Although Merrill Benfield grew up in York, South Carolina, a small upcountry town that has been supplying cotton to the international trade since before the American Revolution, he acquired worldly taste at an early age. His father's cotton mills specialized in custom-dyed textiles, and the son quickly learned from him about the myriad shades of color fabric can be dyed, as well as the differences among various weaves and compositions of finished cloth. From his mother, an antiques aficionado who advised on furniture selections for the Kennedy White House, he inherited a passion for antique furniture. Traveling with her on buying trips, he learned at a young age to identify the various French and English styles and to appreciate the luxurious finishes of eighteenth- and nineteenth-century furniture.

It is not surprising that Merrill became an antiques collector himself, making payments on a fine George II bookcase and Regency sideboard in his twenties. He also became an interior decorator, relocating to Charleston, where he easily found clients who required his expert eye. Merrill is also a collector of vintage automobiles, including an exquisite Silver Dawn (a rare and sought after Rolls Royce model), and seven other classic cars. When he began looking for a home for himself in Charleston, his requirements included elegant architecture, a yard large enough to accommodate his car collection, and rooms that would provide the proper setting for his favorite antiques, including the bookcase and the sideboard.

ABOVE: Merrill used this early-twentieth-century export carpet from China to establish a simple palette for the living room, based on shades of taupe, sky blue, and cobalt. The restrained form and patterning of the Roman blinds and the ivory leather upholstery on the English Chippendale sofa help to balance the more highly charged objects in the room.

OPPOSITE: Made for export to America and Europe, early-twentieth-century Chinese carpets were popular in Charleston and are gaining in value today. Their bold forms and large fields of color add interest to rooms, contrasting with, yet complementing English, American, and European furniture, such as this nineteenth-century French chair.

LEFT: This English Regency chandelier of alabaster and bronze shows off to advantage against the dining room's sky-blue ceiling and simple corona medallion. When illuminated, the alabaster globes cast a rosy, amber glow against the room's shiny brown walls.

OPPOSITE: Merrill paid homage to the design genius of Billy Baldwin in his dining room, painting the walls a lacquer-like chocolate shade, mirroring the mantel, and hanging simple cotton duck curtains. The simple yet elegant setting provides the perfect backdrop for Merrill's beautifully carved Regency sideboard and alabaster and bronze chandelier.

In 1995, he and a friend pulled up in a vintage Bentley Continental Coupe alongside an aging architectural gem—an 1830s Greek Revival-style single house with a large side yard and intact carriage house, where the Silver Dawn and the Bentley convertible are now in residence. Although it had been closed up for forty years, much of the house's original material remained, including a tight corkscrew staircase that twists through the center of the house, cypress door and window surrounds, and spare, early Greek Revival moldings. "Two years in the money pit resulted in the re-creation of a jewel of Charleston architecture," says Merrill of the project that included rebuilding the piazzas, chimneys, windows and hiring a Connecticut-based restoration contractor to restore the corkscrew staircase.

Like many Charleston single houses of this period, the rooms, though beautifully proportioned, are not large. Merrill's goal was to furnish them to function both for comfortable at-home living as well as for frequent entertainments. The first floor drawing room illustrates the ease with which the designer met the challenge. Rather than pushing the room's sofa and chairs out to the room's edges, which makes conversation and the passing of hors d'oeuvres and cocktails a challenge, he created an intimate seating area in front of the room's working fireplace.

He achieved this by floating a large English Chippendale sofa, upholstered in tufted ivory leather, in the middle of the room and placing a pair of French armchairs on either side of the fireplace.

Since he often works at home, he added a Regency desk to the room's furnishings, placing it directly behind the sofa and adding an antique Chippendale armchair where he can sit and complete his correspondence. The George II bookcase dominates one wall of the room, filled with antique volumes Merrill inherited. To these typical Anglo-European furnishings, he added a wide range of decorative objéts that have led him to call this room the United Nations of Style room.

"It truly has something from nearly every nation, including Zuni Indian pottery," he explains. A tall Russian clock with ivory and turquoise panels stands in one corner and a French Empire chandelier hangs above an early-twentieth-century Chinese carpet. A Tiffany bronze fire screen that

was given to Merrill's mother by an aunt stands in front of the fireplace, flanked by a French empire console standing on a gilded base with a triple dolphin motif. Chinese and English bronzes stand on brightly polished surfaces next to Irish crystal, English silver, and Italian marble.

"Some people in Charleston want a strictly Federal room, or a French room, but I find that different things from around the world, made in varied styles and periods, breathe life into a room that is lively and harmonious," says Merrill, explaining his eclectic aesthetic. In order to create a soft backdrop for the many high-impact objects in the room, Merrill painted the walls and moldings in two shades of rose-infused taupe. For the first few years of his residence, he enjoyed opulent swag-and-bow

curtains of Scalamandré silk, but one day he walked in and decided that he wanted something simpler. "With a martini, a cigar, and a stepladder, I had them down in ten minutes," he recalls. Since then, he has replaced them with simple Roman blinds of tan and taupe silk that reveal the windows' hand-carved cypress surrounds. Today, the room's palette reflects that of the 1920s Chinese export carpet on the floor, with shades of taupe, sky blue, and cobalt. This simplified color scheme and window treatment allows the room's exquisite objects to shine.

Merrill chose an equally restrained approach to designing the dining room across the hall. Here, inspired by Billy Baldwin, he painted the walls a deeply glazed shade of brown and hung plain cotton duck curtains from two windows. "It is a dark room and at first I fought that, painting it various shades that I thought would enliven it. But once I decided to let it be a dark room, with dark walls, it all came together," says Merrill. A pale blue ceiling brings an illusion of light into the room and provides a cool background for the glowing alabaster and bronze English regency chandelier that hangs above the table. Mirrored panels (another idea borrowed from Billy Baldwin) surround the fireplace and more mirrors decorate the backs of French doors that open into the kitchen next door.

Merrill's Regency sideboard forms a massive and elegant focal point to the room that is decorated with a combination of French and English antiques and Asian decorative objects. The dining table is an English piece Merrill discovered in Virginia while participating in a road rally. Stopping off at an antique shop, he purchased the long table and broke it down into twelve pieces that he could fit in his yellow Lincoln Continental convertible before completing the race. French painted and upholstered drawing room chairs inherited from his mother stand at the head of the table, which is

surrounded by Chinese Chippendale chairs with melon-colored leather seats the designer found in an antiques store. Chinese porcelains gleam from the illuminated china cabinets the designer had built on either side of the mirrored mantel, and a Chinese painting hangs above the fireplace.

While the dining room's mélange of furnishings and objects reflects an eighteenth- and nine-teenth-century approach to chinoiserie, the master bedroom celebrates the late-nineteenth-century orientalism of Delacroix, who scoured Arabic lands in search of exotic inspiration. Here, orientalist paintings of Bedouins hang on walls painted a deep shade of pimento that turns a rich burnt umber at night. A Chinese Chippendale bed with an elaborately carved cornice forms a centerpiece. For window treatments, the designer selected a red paisley Persian pattern from Scalamandré, edged with tea-dyed linen to give them a modern air.

The most surprising room in the house is the summer bedroom, a chamber located on the top floor of the house. "I wanted a room that was both totally over the top but also that offered a quiet alternative to the rest of the house," says Merrill.

OPPOSITE: The inspiration for this master bedroom's color scheme came from the orientalist paintings (French, nineteenth-century) of Bedouins. Merrill painted the walls an intense shade of red that appears pimento bright in the daylight, but darkens to a rich burnt umber at night. A very fine Chippendale bed with a carved and pierced gallery is another focal point in this room. Curtains of a paisley pattern from Scalamandré add yet more detail.

"The fantasy of a tented room occurred to me, but after speaking with several faux-finishers about painting the walls to resemble tent panels, I decided to make it a real tent." To this end, Merrill hired a local upholsterer who required two weeks and three hundred yards of ticking to create the fantasy tent room. "The idea was to create a peaceful sanctuary at the back of the house, where there was no noise, and where I could read at night and wake up to ultimate simplicity."

There is no television or radio in this room—not even a telephone. Books fill the built-in shelves and simple furnishings line the room. The bed has an upholstered headboard of red-and-white toile that contrasts nicely with the black-and-white ticking tent. A French Empire chest, chosen for its contrasting wood veneer surfaces, stands against one wall. In a tented corner, a chair with lemon yellow upholstery offers comfortable seating next to a table stacked with books. A mirrored French art deco dressing table fills one of the dormer window spaces, reflecting the ticked fabric in geometrically inspired angles. "I love to wake up in this room," says Merrill. "Here, in its ultimate simplicity, I can prepare my mind for the day."

OPPOSITE: In contrast to the exuberant orientalism of the master bedroom, this tented room, which serves both as an alternate bedroom for Merrill and as a guest room, offers a soothing retreat. Merrill designed this room with the goal of quieting his senses and his mind after a day's work in order to awake refreshed and creatively recharged.

ACCIDENTAL MODERNISTS

A REMODELED
NINETEENTH-CENTURY WAREHOUSE
The Home of James and Miss Ray Coker

James and Miss Ray Coker both grew up in the midst of old South Carolina families, surrounded by classic furniture, portraits, and plenty of inherited bric-a-brac. Both clung to their aesthetic traditions for the first halves of their lives, becoming accidental modernists only a decade or so ago when they contracted architect W. G. Clark to renovate their Charleston home on Bedon's Alley. They hired the die-hard modernist, a University of Pennsylvania trained devotee of Louis Kahn and Carlo Scarpa, at the suggestion of their friend, Charleston-based designer Sherry Taylor. Although the project was filled with emotionally fraught skirmishes on subjects ranging from aesthetics and architecture to proportion and preservation, the final result expresses both the timeless serenity of Charleston and calming purity of Modernist architecture.

Like many other Charleston houses, including the one that Miss Ray lived up in on South Adgers Wharf, the structure on Bedon's Alley began life as a utilitarian building. Both homes were built as warehouses for the goods that passed through Charleston's busy eighteenth- and nineteenth-century port. When the port suffered setbacks in the second half of the nineteenth century, many such buildings were converted into residences, including the 1781 barrel factory on Bedon's Alley. Remodeled in the late Victorian age to resemble a Charleston single house, the building's large interior spaces were divided into a warren of small rooms and its large exterior doorways

PREVIOUS PAGE: Ruddy brick, cool bluestone, and golden stucco create an interplay of colors and textures in the entrance court of the Cokers' home, a renovated eighteenth-century warehouse in the heart of historic Charleston. Steel-cased windows and doors visually unite the two parts of the building, which include the original brick structure and a modern addition at its rear.

LEFT: Clark explored the Modernist principle of transparency throughout the house, balancing reassuringly solid materials including concrete and brick with open doorways and walls of glass that dissolve the barriers between rooms and indoor and outdoor spaces.

OPPOSITE: Surfaces of concrete, glass, and steel create a modern kitchen area where glimpses of the surrounding older houses and brick walls can be seen through transparent walls. W. G. Clark designed the room's minimalist furniture using mahogany, in a nod to Charleston's traditional wood of choice.

were refashioned into domestically scaled windows equipped with louvered shutters. Within the rooms, layers of ceilings and wall surfaces were applied to bare bricks and rough wood surfaces, and more rooms were added to the back of the house.

At first, Clark refused to take on the project, assuming that the Cokers wanted only to spruce up the nineteenth-century conversion without embracing a thoroughly Modernist makeover. Quoted in the *New York Times* as declaring, "We are modern architects; we abhor anything else," Clark was not willing to compromise. But it turned out that the Cokers were and the two parties finally agreed to work together. "We had very little knowledge about things modern in architecture, and we learned some things and fell in love with what

we learned," explains Miss Ray, adding that Clark, former chairman of the University of Virginia's architecture department, is "a wonderful educator." Working with the architect, the couple finally settled on a plan to return the old warehouse to its original shape, open-plan form, and simple materials, and to replace the wooden addition at its rear with an unapologetically modern one of modern glass, concrete, and steel.

While the Cokers' decision shocked some of their more conservative neighbors, this readiness to accept new styles and apply them to older buildings is actually quite in keeping with Charleston's architectural history. Over the centuries, well-to-do homeowners have frequently revamped Georgian houses in Adamesque styles or added Greek revival

details or additions to Federal homes. But in late-twentieth-century Charleston, where preservation became the obsession of residents fighting to protect their antique architectural heritage from demolition and decay, the embrace of modern design had come to be viewed as sacrilege. So when Clark presented his plans for the modernist makeover for approval to the city's Board of Architectural Review, a horde of neighbors showed up to protest.

While such grass roots protests have helped make Charleston a city with the best preserved eighteenth- and nineteenth-century architecture and urban fabric in America, they also negate the fluidity with which its original inhabitants absorbed and expressed changing tastes. Julie Iovine, architectural critic for the *New York Times,* described this impulse

as "a local obsession with making the city more eighteenth century than it was in the eighteenth century." Such battles between architects and preservationists have become common in present-day Charleston, and the results are mixed.

Often, truly inappropriately scaled or detailed designs are scuttled to the overall benefit of the urban whole. Other times, potentially innovative new buildings, renovations, and additions end up bland shadows of their original designs, frustrating architects and residents who wish to advance Charleston's ongoing style evolution. In the past, many buildings that should not have been demolished have been, and others that should have been scratched on the drawing board have come to unfortunate fruition. The Cokers' residence represents

OPPOSITE: A steel trellis projects above the bay of glass and steel that encloses the kitchen sitting area. It was designed to support vines of Carolina jasmine and Noisette roses, two traditional flowers favored by old Charlestonians. Although the flowers refused to flourish there, the curving silhouette of the trellis softens the façade and echoes the shapes of surrounding tree limbs.

LEFT: The bluestone terrace wraps around the house, creating a tiny courtyard at the rear just large enough for an ornamental tree and a wall fountain.

the best outcome of this dialogue—a slightly modified project that successfully integrates elements of the old and the new, thus respecting the past while creating something innovative and of its time.

"The three of us suddenly came to the idea that less was going to be better than more in this house," says James, recalling a critical moment in the design process. "Everything in the original brick building would be just as it was when it was a barrel warehouse. But the addition would be purely modern, with steel, glass, and concrete." This was the part of the project that caused greatest consternation among neighbors, even though it was largely hidden behind a wall. Although the final design was scaled back a bit, the addition still maintains a distinctly contemporary appearance. "It was amazing to discover how the very contemporary addition blended perfectly with the eighteenth-century original," says James of the final result. Today, a minimalist courtyard hidden from the

street by a brick wall stretches beside the house where an old fashioned garden once bloomed. Edged with camellias, the bluestone-paved terrace terminates in a rectangular reflecting pool whose dark surface echoes the graceful forms of overarching trees. The warehouse's brick façade is punctuated with tall apertures fitted with steel mullioned doors and louvered shutters similar to those used on nearby houses. At the rear of the house, the brick masonry dissolves into a wall of golden stucco and a bay of glass and steel that sheaths the modern addition.

The house's main entrance opens into the juncture between the old and the new. To the right of the entrance, a wall of sandblasted glass forms a translucent curtain between a new mahogany staircase climbing to the second floor and a contemporary kitchen. Built-in furniture of mahogany (a material Clark selected in tribute to Charleston's past) creates a minimalist sitting area in the plate glass bay

TOP LEFT: A Gothic Chippendale style chair shares one of the large entertaining room's sitting areas with contemporary armchairs. Family heirlooms, including a late-eighteenth-century portrait of a child and a tall case clock, and a contemporary painting by Charleston artist Douglas Balentine create a harmonious eclecticism.

TOP RIGHT: Golden travertine marble now paves the warehouse's first floor room where arrangements of furniture suggest discrete zones for gathering and dining. Delicately proportioned contemporary chairs and an antique table evoke the simple elegance of early-nineteenth-century furniture in the dining area. A Rough-hewn wooden side table by contemporary designer Holly Hunt creates lively contrast with an elegant Venetian glass mirror.

OPPOSITE: The second-story room's floor is covered with glowing boards of deep red mahogany carpeted in areas with luxurious carpets. A large interior window in the rear wall of the room frames a view of the iron spiral staircase that serves as a visual bridge from the old part of the house to the new, as well as a tangible bridge to the third floor attic.

overlooking the reflecting pool. This area, called the vitrine, is James' favorite place to sit, whether working at a laptop computer or enjoying evening meals with his wife. "I feel like I'm inside and outside at the same time when I sit there," he says.

An antique Chinese vase of blue and white porcelain stands on the modern mahogany table. More heirlooms inhabit the long room on the far side of the staircase, a large entertaining area that fills the ground floor of the original structure. A late-eighteenth-century portrait of a young girl hangs above the fireplace in a sitting area occupied by modern upholstered pieces. A Venetian mirror fills the space between two steel-and-glass doors. Contemporary chairs with backs of cherry reminiscent of a simplified Chippendale design surround an early-nineteenth-century American banquet table in the dining area. "We've found that in many cases, the eighteenth- and early-nineteenth-century pieces go so well with the modern pieces," notes James.

Clusters of furniture and carpeted areas divide the large space into three zones: two sitting areas and one for dining. The upstairs room of the original warehouse structure is similarly divided, with eclectic arrangements of furniture and art suggesting lines of demarcation. A grisaille eighteenth-century French chair, selected by designer Sherry Taylor and upholstered in Italian tie silk, adds a traditional note to the contemporary upholstered pieces in the sitting area. An American Empire pedestal table separates this area from the "bedroom." The bed's tall headboard serves as a divider separating the rest of the room from the library, where books on contemporary art and architecture share shelves with historical tomes on South Carolina.

Like eighteenth- and nineteenth-century houses that were built without closets, this room offered no storage for clothing, so the Cokers purchased an antique chest-on-chest for that purpose. "It's one of the few times that a piece of antique furniture is still actually used for what it was designed," James notes. Storage space and a large master bath are located in the modern addition to the second floor, which is visible through two openings in the wall at the rear of the large room. One open doorway leads to the light-filled stair hall. The other frames a view of an iron spiral staircase that leads to the attic floor. This curving form, bathed by natural light from the courtyard, creates a dramatic, sculptural element visually linking the old part of the house with the new.

After growing up in houses where rooms were treated as distinct, enclosed spaces, the Cokers wondered whether they might find life in their newly renovated house challenging. "We thought we might feel vulnerable living in these big, open rooms," says Miss Ray. "But instead," James says, "the thickness of the walls and the very Zen nature of the space gives you a very secure feeling. I love the simplicity and economy of materials. I'm making great steps towards being a less-is-best sort of clean, classical person." Fortunately, some of the neighbors have come around, too, recognizing the Modernist makeover in their midst as a turn-of-the-twentieth-century Charleston classic.

OPPOSITE: Modern furniture and art, a Moorish bedside table, a nineteenth-century American chest-on-chest, and Chinese ceramics blend in serene eclecticism in the upstairs room thanks to the simplicity of line they share and an elegantly neutral palette.

SILK PURSE

A RENOVATED 1740s SLAVE QUARTERS
The Home of Eve and Jon Blossom

Charleston's first European settlers were entrepreneurial types: hopeful newcomers with big dreams and unlimited ingenuity. They were also citizens of the world, transatlantic travelers whose circles of trade stretched from Africa to the Far East. The city's outstanding natural harbor and its fertile soil were among the key attractions that drew such people to Charleston in the seventeenth and eighteenth centuries. Today, the city continues to attract new citizens, not only because of its gentle climate and natural beauty, but also because of the architectural and cultural legacy left by its founders. Many of these newcomers reconnect the strands of the city's bold and global past with the present, planting new dreams in old soil and bringing new style to antique houses.

Eve and Jon Blossom, who moved to Charleston from San Francisco in 2000, are such new Charlestonians. Eve chose Charleston as the home for her start-up business, Lulan Artisans, a textile company featuring silk and organic cotton hand-dyed and woven in five Southeast Asian countries. Jon uses the city as a home base for his work as a designer of interactive computer software products for clients across the country. Together, they have restored a 1740s slave quarter building, retaining all the original material that was salvageable, while installing twenty-first-century technology behind ceilings and walls. "I love the idea of hiding state-of-the-art technology inside an antique package," says Jon.

Tucked off Philadelphia Alley, a cobblestone pedestrian byway in the middle of historic downtown

OPPOSITE: The Blossoms' circa 1740 house is tucked down a brick and stone paved alley in downtown Charleston. Originally, the two-story pink building served as slave quarters for a larger house that stood on the far side of the courtyard paralleling the alley.

ABOVE: The Blossoms' house is secluded from vehicular and even much pedestrian traffic, bordered by a private courtyard, Philadelphia Alley, and the cemetery of St. Philip's Church.

OPPOSITE: The living room reveals the addition of Federal style architectural details, including plain wainscoting, a neoclassical mantel, and window surrounds, after the slave quarter was transformed into more upscale housing. Bright red art deco club chairs, Asian furniture, including an Indonesian ottoman, and a collection of international art and artifacts offsets the formality of the room's architectural details.

ABOVE: East and West meet in this room, where an art deco English tea service sits on an Indonesian ottoman. Contemporary textiles designed in America and woven in Asia for Lulan Artisans, including the ottoman's silk upholstery and the lustrous carpet, add modern notes.

Charleston, the small masonry dwelling faces a private courtyard on one side and an old cemetery on another. "As soon as you turn down the alley, it's cool and quiet. You are in this oasis—no cars, no noises except the sound of church bells, trees everywhere, and houses that haven't been changed for more than a century. There is nothing to tell you it's not 1800," says Jon. "It's a calming respite from the rest of the world," adds Eve.

Eve and Jon also chose the house because much of its early building materials were still intact, including wide pine floorboards, mantels, doors, and window surrounds added when the austere slave quarters were transformed into more upscale housing following the Civil War. Rather than attempt to restore the house to any particular period, the Blossoms chose to remove as much inferior surface material as possible, replacing missing or damaged wood with heart pine recycled from old buildings and using environmentally-friendly paints and finishes.

The final result celebrates the original masonry exterior walls, Federal style mantels probably transplanted from another Charleston home in the nineteenth century, and interior window surrounds dating from a 1940s Colonial revival makeover. This kind of architectural collage is typical of Charleston dwellings that have housed residents over centuries of sociological and aesthetic change. While the interior design of the former slave quarters appears, at first, to be done in a modern global-eclectic vein, it, too, reflects Charleston's eclectic approach to style. "Because the house is traditional in appearance, we felt that the furniture should complement that, so we used a mix of American, English, and Asian furniture, just as eighteenth- and nineteenth-century Charlestonians did," explains Eve.

In those days, the city's wealthy citizens decorated their homes primarily with furniture made by local artisans or imported from England or New York and set their tables with silver from England, crystal from Ireland, and porcelain from China. Unlike

TOP LEFT: The kitchen's floor is fashioned from antique pine and topped with a modern countertop material called Silestone, formed from quartz. Blown-glass lamp shades lend a warm glow to the room, echoed by the saffron-colored cubbyholes housing souvenirs from favorite travel destinations.

TOP RIGHT: Ming-style cabinets painted pistachio green, a 1950s floor lamp, and a contemporary Vietnamese painting create an eclectic retreat for guests. Textiles from Lulan Artisans in shades of blue and gray complement the prevailing green of the room's décor.

these early Charlestonians, who rarely traveled in the eastern hemisphere, Eve has voyaged widely in Southeast Asia and lived in Vietnam, where she worked as an architect. Jon has also traveled in Asia, where the two have collected ceramics, wood carvings, basketry, and artworks that they display in their Charleston home. These objects share space in their home with western antiques and contemporary furniture. Textiles from Eve's company provide the thread that connects these disparate elements and helps them blend with their architectural setting. "The textiles, which look both contemporary and traditional, tie it all together," explains Eve.

A Federal style mantel, plain wainscoting, and deep-set windows create an old-fashioned Charleston look in the Blossom's living room. But the decorations lend an exotic note, including an Indonesian ottoman upholstered in lustrous red silk made by Lulan and travel souvenirs from Nepal, Burma, and New Zealand. A pair of art deco club chairs from England, still covered with original red leather, and an art deco tea set add twentieth-century verve. A hand-knotted silk runner made by Lulan traverses the floor, its pattern pulling together the geometric motifs in the furnishings and architecture.

In the dining room, Eve and Jon painted the walls a serene shade reminiscent of wet clay, using an environmentally friendly line of paint from Sherwin Williams called Horizon. Against this restful backdrop, contemporary paintings from Vietnam and an art nouveau pendant lamp from Czechoslovakia offer boldly calligraphic silhouettes. While the elegantly restrained dining table dates from the late eighteenth century, Eve often sets it with a cherished collection of celadon-colored Depression glass.

A pair of curvy scroll-back chairs upholstered in puckered silk from Lulan adds an opulent touch to the room. "There is something about the way the cloth's texture and graduated stripes look on those chairs that everybody loves," says Eve. A table runner (also from her company) unites the greenish-turquoise tones of the chairs and Depression glass with the clay color of the wall. Sheer silk organza window panels woven in Thailand with a raised pattern of diamonds filter the light and contribute further elegance to the space.

These two entertaining rooms are linked by a Pullman-style kitchen designed by Eve and two Charleston-based architects, Beau Clowney and Sam Furr, to get maximum utility out of the small space. Black Silestone counters and stainless steel appliances create a contemporary appearance, while hand-blown pendant lamps recall art nouveau taste. A row of illuminated cubbyholes painted a deep shade of saffron displays more of the couple's souvenirs from Asia and a window over the sink frames a view of the cemetery next door.

A campaign bed that belonged to a brigadier general during the War of 1812 takes center stage in the master bedroom on the house's second floor. Designed to be set up and broken down easily during camp movements, the bed's lightweight wood components are marked with Roman numerals. Luminous silk woven with alternating bands of opaque and sheer fabric covers the delicate arch of the canopy. A duvet cover featuring asymmetrical vertical stripes in complementary tones adds subtle vibrancy to the bedding, as do throw pillows clad in a variety of patterns and colors. Shifting greenery seen through sheer curtain panels creates an airy, tropical atmosphere and a runner of lustrous silk carpet adds an opulent touch to this treetop-high nest.

Unlike guest rooms that feel like an afterthought, the Blossoms' is actually larger than their master bedroom. It is also equally bedecked with silk textiles, including a blue silk duvet cover, a tasseled throw in taupe-toned silk, and throw pillows in several shades and patterns. The room's cool palette of green and blue and the pure lines of Asian furniture, including a mahogany bed with rattan panels and Ming-style bedside tables, create a serene retreat that is the most contemporary and most Asian-leaning of the rooms.

The Blossoms' approach to layering styles, periods, and international influences in this antique building is consistent with Charleston's design ethos. But it is the ubiquitous fabrics from Eve's company that create the most fascinating link to Charleston's past. In a way, these textiles are a contemporary equivalent to antique Chinese export ware—porcelains made in China with styles designed to appeal to fashion-conscious Western consumers. Such export ware came to Charleston by the boatload in the eighteenth and early nineteenth century.

The fabrics also serve as a reminder that two of the agricultural products linked to Charleston's fortune—sea island cotton and indigo—were used in manufacturing textiles. Finally, the textiles recall the city's tradition of exquisite artisanship, as refined by its furniture makers, silversmiths, and other decorative artists. Eve and Jon both share this sense of fine craftsmanship and dedication to design, using these attributes to transform this former slave quarter into a true silk purse of a house.

OPPOSITE: An 1810 campaign bed lends a British colonial air to the master bedroom, which Eve decorated liberally with silks from her company, including the bed's canopy, duvet cover, pillows and striped carpet.

58

THE
·JAMES VERREE HOUSE·

This Pre-Revolutionary
single house is one of a group
of three dwellings including 56
and 60 Church Street, built c.
1794 by Jonah Verree, a house
carpenter. The Verree House
was purchased in 1814 by
Thomas Heyward, a signer of
the Declaration of Independence.
The garden was designed by
noted landscape architect
Loutrel Briggs in 1942 and was
considered his favorite garden.

CHARLESTON CHARM

THE JAMES VEREE HOUSE
*The Home of Charles and Marty Whaley
Adams Cornwell*

By virtue of both birth and upbringing, artist and garden-writer Marty Whaley Adams Cornwell is steeped in Charleston charm. Her mother was Emily Whaley, author of the runaway best-selling gardening memoir, *Mrs. Whaley and Her Charleston Garden*, which describes one of the city's most cherished private gardens. In addition to tending her garden and raising three daughters, Mrs. Whaley also taught dancing and social graces to several generations of Charleston children. Marty's father, attorney Ben Scott Whaley, devoted his energies to protecting Charleston's historic architecture as a long-time president of Historic Charleston Foundation. Among the buildings he helped rescue is the Nathaniel Russell House, one of the city's most graceful mansions.

Marty and her sisters were born and raised in a Georgian house in the antique residential neighborhood referred to as "South of Broad." The plainly detailed center-hall house, with compact rooms and walls of unadorned plaster and cypress paneling, was built circa 1745 by a Quaker named James Veree. Veree's son sold the house to Thomas Heyward, a signer of the Declaration of Independence, who may have used it as a rental property. Marty's father bought it in 1938, and the house still remains in the family, eight decades later. "I don't think Mama and Daddy realized what a treasure this house was," muses Marty. "They just bought it to live in. Now I think we have a better appreciation for the fact that cities like Charleston and New Orleans can practically disappear overnight—

OPPOSITE: The severe simplicity of the façade of Marty Whaley Adams and Charles Cornwell's house, built circa 1745 by a Quaker, gives little hint of the ebullient style that finds expression within the rooms and the garden behind it.

ABOVE: A central stair hall of painted cypress rises through three stories of the house. Bright rooms on the front of the house are illuminated by tall windows on three sides. Marty chose a warm palette of amber, rose, and gold for the drawing room that seems to glow in the light that pours in through the windows.

TOP LEFT: The original cypress paneling of the central stair hall has been painted white as long as Marty can remember. She embellished it with montage, mounting old prints of Italian architecture on the walls, and delicate stenciling reminiscent of Swedish country style.

TOP MIDDLE: Curtains of damask, dyed amber, soften the light that flows into this room from tall windows. Gilt on cornice boards, picture frames, and mirrors add gold's bright gleam to the sunny room.

TOP RIGHT: Marty created curtain tiebacks from a collection of brass finger bowls her great-great-aunts bought during their travels. She mounted them on wooden knobs found at a hardware store and attached them to the wall.

OPPOSITE: A comfortably eclectic array of furniture including a chintz-covered sofa and chairs with fraying upholstery occupies the drawing room. A large needlepoint carpet unifies the colors in the room. Marty's paintings hang on the walls and gleaming cornice boards that she designed and gilded support floor to ceiling curtains of damask.

ABOVE: A bamboo table, French armchair, and Italian painted commode coexist in easy eclectic style in Marty's drawing room.

OPPOSITE LEFT: A dog portrait by Marty hangs above the mantel like a genial ancestor in the formal dining rooms whose walls were once covered by an inch-thick layer of old wallpapers. Once these were removed, Marty painted the plaster above the cypress wainscoting a shade of lavender to complement the room's dark mahogany furniture, silver accoutrements, and blue-and-white Canton china.

OPPOSITE RIGHT: Marty upholstered dining chairs and an Empire style sofa (not seen) in ivory leather, adding a touch of sophistication and sensuality to the Old World room. The triple-tiered tea table in the room's corner has stood there, covered with family silver, since Marty was a child.

that old, charming places like these are unique and irreplaceable!"

When Marty inherited the house upon the settlement of her mother's estate, she was a little wary of moving back into the home where she had grown up. Although of late, lots of well-to-do newcomers from "off"—as Charlestonians call anyone who is not from the city—have moved to the neighborhood south of Broad Street, it is still hallowed ground to locals. This is where they remember playing hide and seek in a maze of old brick walls tangled with scented vines, attending dancing school wearing frills or bow ties and white gloves, and later, waltzing and fox-trotting at debutante parties.

While such traditions are fondly cherished, they can also be overwhelming, bringing with them equal measures of nostalgia and anxiety. Even though Charlestonians of the early twentieth century did not necessarily have a lot of money, there was a great deal of social aplomb required to maintain the accepted status quo. While eccentricity was tolerated, conformity was preferred. Houses had relatively predictable décor, heavy on American and English antiques, and often light on individual style. So when Marty, a divorced mother of two and an artist who had previously lived over her Meeting Street gallery, faced the prospect of moving back into her family's home, she felt a little nervous.

"I just wasn't sure how I was going to make this house my own home—a place where I could be completely comfortable and be myself." Five years and a major addition and renovation project later, the house is finally becoming what Marty hoped it would be for her and her second husband, writer

OPPOSITE: Marty covered the walls of this informal dining room, created during the remodeling of the house, with parchment colored Venetian plaster, immediately lending a sense of age to the space. A pierced brass Moroccan lantern and an iron and glass garden chandelier offer more informal lighting than chandeliers but more charm than recessed lighting.

TOP LEFT: Two tall, arched French doors open in the wall of the informal living room onto shallow iron balconies overlooking the garden. Marty covered the walls of this room with dark gray Venetian plaster—a cool tone that complements the verdant view through the windows.

TOP MIDDLE: Added during the remodeling of the house, this master bedroom opens through French doors onto a balcony overlooking the garden. An antique plantation bed—a family heirloom—and a French daybed painted white provide plenty of opportunity to sit back and relax. More family heirlooms, including a tall chest-on-chest, also decorate this room with a view.

TOP RIGHT: A reproduction of Rodin's bust of a young girl adds a charming detail to a corner of the cypress-lined stair hall that ascends through the house's center. Stenciled garlands and sepia-toned prints applied to the walls conjure an Old World European mood in this space.

TOP LEFT: Marty transformed a small sitting room on the second floor of the house into an office for her husband, writer and editor Charles Cornwell. Although little natural light comes into this room, which is on the side of the house, she created a warm glow by having the original cypress paneling and shelves stripped back to their original light brown shade and covering the remaining walls with Venetian plaster in a shade of Pompeian red.

TOP RIGHT: Sumptuous red-and-bronze brocade curtains, blood red plaster, warm wood, and gleaming gilt and brass details create a masculine retreat in Charles' office, where an antique globe and a portrait of his mother sit upon his large desk.

and editor Charles Cornwell. "When I decorate a house, I try to create a second skin. I want people to walk in and feel that they know something about who I am. I think when people come into this house now, they feel something about my essence, and also about the essence of Charleston."

"This house is positively encased in charm," a recent visitor exclaimed, trying to capture this essence in words. Defining charm, Marty explains, "A charming person knows how to make people feel at home, putting them at ease, inspiring them, and embracing them. A kind of embrace—this is what a charming house does, too. You want to go in and devour it with your eyes and your senses. You want to stay for awhile and explore more about the person who made it. You wonder, how did they create it? Can any of it ooze back into me?"

Reflecting upon her upbringing, Marty identifies some of the elements of her signature style, which celebrates the touch of the hand, the use of imagination, and the patina and texture of well-loved, well-worn objects. "The Charleston I grew up in did not have a lot of lavish spending," she recalls. "Sometimes, if we didn't have something we wanted, we just made it ourselves. To me, making do is sometimes way more attractive than buying the most expensive things." A perfect example is the curtain tiebacks she fashioned for the windows in the front parlor.

This room, which had a formal color scheme of gray and burgundy in Marty's childhood days, has now been made over in glowing shades of amber and cream. Twenty-year-old damask curtains from her mother's era, dyed warm gold, soften the room's seven windows. They are held open by antique brass finger bowls mounted on wooden knobs, their embossed convex bases gleaming like little golden domes. "Those finger bowls came

from my great-great-aunts, who did a huge amount of traveling and brought home wonderful things," says Marty, who also mounted majolica plates they collected in Italy in her back parlor and recently restored some of their table linens.

Like her aunts, Marty also loves to travel and shop for ideas and items for her house. Several trips to Italy informed her palette, sparking a passion for walls of deeply textured plaster and shades of sienna, burnt umber, and deep terra-cotta. Marty took several courses in decorative paint techniques so she could re-create the texture and color of Venetian plaster at home. Having toured Sweden when she was twenty-one, she also loves Swedish style. Inspired by books on the subject, she borrowed the idea of embellishing walls with delicate stenciled garlands and painting and glazing wood surfaces pale shades that reflect the light. "One of the boldest things I did in this house was to refinish all the old dark pine floors with a sheer pinkish-white glaze," she says.

A trip to Morocco sparked an interest in arabesque patterns, which Marty has incorporated into her wall decorations. She also bought several pierced metal lanterns to illuminate a new dining room that fills a large bay of windows added to the side of the house in the renovation project. While such a global approach to decoration may seem out of place in downtown Charleston, actually eighteenth- and nineteenth-century Charlestonians loved Italian art and architecture, and Marty explains that her great-grandmother possessed a Moroccan lantern that hung in a corner of her parlor. "I think if my mother's generation had access to the same kind of beautiful style books we have today, they would have been much more adventurous," she adds.

However, early-twentieth-century Charleston style was largely informed by the city's own past, with homeowners decorating primarily with the antiques they inherited and adhering to the city's traditional tastes. Blue and white was the color scheme of choice, as illustrated in the old dining room in Marty's house, where forty-year-old blue and white curtains and three-hundred-year-old blue Canton china define the palette. During the renovation, Marty discovered layer upon layer of old wallpaper, all in patterns of blue and white, dating back to the earliest decoration of the room. The oldest layer is glued to muslin that was nailed to the cypress walls when the house was built. Marty plans to develop a stencil using some of the motifs from the old wallpapers to decorate the room's walls, which are now painted a deep silvery

shade of violet. "I loved the idea of decorating a room in shades of violet and silver," says Marty. "But I also wanted to keep the blue-and-white details that have always been there."

The original house was modest in size, with two rooms on each floor opening off a small central stair hall. Because the houses in Charleston's old residential neighborhoods are so close together, the rooms often tend to be a bit dark and can feel a bit cramped. "I needed to open up, lighten up, and twirl and dance and fly though the house," says Marty, who hired consultant Chip Laurens to enlarge the house. In addition to adding the airy dining bay, they remodeled the first floor to include a living room at the back of the house with French doors that open to the garden. "We never had

enough access to the garden," recalls Marty of her childhood days in the house.

Marty painted this room a matte shade of gray Venetian plaster resembling slate that complements the cool green vistas of the garden that now take center stage. Above this room is a new master bedroom, decorated in shades of summer sunlight—with pale apricot walls, warm beige and amber textiles, and dark honey-colored antiques. This room has two French doors as well, opening out to a balcony that provides the perfect vantage point for viewing the garden.

The garden was designed in the 1940s by Loutrel Briggs, who was the foremost landscape architect in twentieth-century Charleston. Briggs created an exquisitely harmonious series of spaces for the long yard, including a rectangular lawn bordered with seasonal blooms, flowering trees, and evergreens, a round reflecting pool, a semicircular walk, and an oval terrace. The plan incorporated borrowed elements including a large oak tree next door and old brick walls and wooden fences. And it has provided nearly eight decades of pleasure and inspiration for Mrs. Whaley and her daughter, Marty.

Mrs. Whaley enjoyed embellishing the garden, adding the old camellias, yews, and hydrangeas that form its skeleton, as well as creating a variety of focal points to charm and delight herself and others. Since inheriting the garden, Marty has simplified it, returning to the clarity of Briggs' plan while exploring new textures and colors in plants. While

she loves the old-fashioned camellias planted by her mother, Marty also enjoys creating unexpected juxtapositions like her early spring plantings of tall white tulips interspersed with darkly ruffling mustard greens. She also created a focal point of her own by mounting a lattice of copper pipe against the back of the house upon which she trained white and lavender blooming vines (native wisteria, passion flower, jasmine, and grape) that create a spicy-sweet bower in the summer.

"I'm as much a set designer as I am a horticulturalist," Marty says. And she might as well add, "or an interior designer." Just as set designers work to create worlds within worlds—spaces where every object is carefully chosen to convey an idea or invoke a mood—so Marty has created a home and a garden that enchant all who enter.

"A charming home is charged with spirit," says Marty. Everyone who visits her house and garden leaves, not only charmed, but recharged and ready to infuse a little more spirit into their own home.

OPPOSITE: Marty and her mother have both enjoyed using containers filled with annuals, such as this stone urn planted with russet pansies, to add more elements of height, shape, color, and texture to the garden.

TOP LEFT: Mossy brick, bright white marble, neatly trimmed boxwood, blossoming camellias, and dangling tendrils of ivy provide a perfect balance of order and natural disarray, creating a garden setting that is infinitely pleasing and comforting.

TOP RIGHT: Planted urns perched upon tall brick posts add eye-level interest in the garden, as do glass lanterns strung from tree limbs. At ground level, neatly trimmed hedges of boxwood lead strolling feet along paths of age-mellowed brick. Many of the camellias are more than fifty years old, lending a full-blown beauty to the garden's perimeter.

OPPOSITE: Marty painted a selection of Victorian-style porch balusters white and attached stakes to their bases. Driven into the garden's soft earth, they support candles that illuminate the garden for nocturnal gatherings.

TOP RIGHT: French doors, balconies, and the outdoor dining area now link the house to the garden. Marty created another visual connection by installing a trellis of copper pipe to the back of the house which is now covered with flowering vines of jasmine, passion flower, and wisteria.

BOTTOM RIGHT: During the remodeling of the house, this outdoor dining area was created so the Cornwells and their friends and family can enjoy meals in the garden during temperate weather. A ceramic wall fountain pours water into a waiting pool, lending a soft burbling sound that is also enjoyed in the living room when the French doors are left ajar.

THE JAMES PETIGRU LAW OFFICE
The Home of Kitty and Irénée May

One of several narrow lanes that crisscross downtown Charleston south of Broad street, St. Michael's Alley is lined with contiguous brick and stucco facades, iron balconies, louvered shutters, and varied rooflines that form a picturesque streetscape. A bustling and prosperous street in the nineteenth century, when lawyers and tradesmen operating businesses amid the middle-class residential tenements, St. Michael's Alley declined into decrepitude in the decades following the Civil War and into the twentieth century. Even so, its romantic appearance attracted the eyes of the artists of the Charleston Renaissance, who frequently rendered it in the early twentieth century.

Undaunted by the ramshackle conditions and noisome odors of the slums that festered in downtown Charleston, Susan Pringle Frost saved this and other parts of old Charleston from neglect and demolition in the nineteen-teens and twenties. Considered the matriarch of the city's preservation movement, Frost bought several houses on St. Michael's Alley and restored them, including the former James Petigru law office, now owned by Kitty and Irénée May. Petigru, a famous Charleston lawyer and statesman, was also not one to shrink

LEFT: The pristine appearance of St. Michael's Alley today offers little reminder of the hurly-burly bustle of business that thronged its sidewalks in the early nineteenth century or the slum-like decay that ensued after the Civil War and into the first decades of the twentieth century.

LEFT: Gilt-edged china and an Old Paris tea set dress the dining room table for afternoon tea. With murals of architectural and landscape scenes from Italy painted on the surrounding walls, the small dining room feels almost like an outdoor dining pavilion in Europe rather than a former law office's waiting room on a narrow Charleston alley.

OPPOSITE: The patterned carpet, pale salmon paint, and swags of striped silk draperies hanging from a gilded curtain pole all lend to the illusion of stepping back into the antebellum South in this entrance hall. A courtly southern gentleman (a resident's ancestor) presides over the hall and a marble-topped console table seems to anticipate the presentation of calling cards.

from difficult challenges. Architectural historian Jonathan Poston, in his volume *The Buildings of Charleston*, describes the one-time attorney general of South Carolina as "Defender of the liberties of the weak, particularly slaves and free blacks" and an opponent to secession.

When present-day resident Kitty May lived across the street in the 1950s, she remembers the street being far less posh than it is today. "The alley was famous because it smelled so badly, and when you drove on it at night, you could hear the crunch of cockroaches," she vividly recollects. Back then, the street was integrated, and poor working class families filled tenements standing next to the homes of old Charleston gentility whose fortunes had waned. Kitty and her now deceased first husband rented a house there while he served at the Charleston naval base. She raised her first child there with the help of an Irish nanny who rented a room across the street in the house that Kitty was to own several decades later.

At that time, three sisters lived in the house, having bought it from Susan Pringle Frost. When the last of the sisters died, the house was offered for auction. Kitty, who was not living in Charleston at the time, heard of the impending sale and decided to make a bid for the house, little dreaming she would actually succeed in buying it. "Everybody wanted that house," she recalls. "Especially lawyers, because of its history and the fact that it was zoned for commercial use."

When Kitty received a call several months later informing her that she had bought the house, she was stunned. "It was falling to bits, and I don't know what we thought we were going to do with it," she recounts. But she and her husband proceeded with the sale and soon began restoring the structure, removing decades' worth of partition walls and flimsy additions to reveal the original shape of the structure.

OPPOSITE: Needlepoint carpets in Aubusson styles cover the floor of the large drawing room that served as law clerks' offices in the mid-nineteenth century. Kitty chose a claret-colored striped wallpaper with a garland border to complement the room's nineteenth-century style. American Empire furniture dominates the room, including two sofas and a pedestal table in the massive, curvilinear style.

RIGHT: A collection of inherited furniture and tableware, including an English table and an American Empire sideboard, several patterns of English and French china, and English silver, decorates the dining room.

In Petigru's time, the front door opened into a side hall with one door leading to a small waiting room (now the dining room) and clerks' office (now the drawing room). The original second floor also included only two rooms: an office for Petigru's nephew (now a library/sitting room) and the lawyer's own large office (now the master bedroom). Once the main rooms had been restored to their original configuration, Kitty, who worked as an interior designer for thirty-five years in Wilmington, Delaware, enjoyed decorating the house.

"The house was built in 1848, and we happened to have inherited a lot of things from that period from two grandmothers on two sides of the family," she says. While Kitty notes that she could have decorated the house in a number of ways, she chose a late-nineteenth-century style with dark mahogany, pale marble, and rich shades of blue and red and gold. "The house seemed to dictate that to me, but also, a lot of my family comes from Natchez, Mississippi, and I love the look of genteel decay that those houses have. I'm a romantic at heart." Throughout its history, the house on St. Michael's Alley seemed to attract romantics, as defined in late-nineteenth-century literature as individuals consumed with passion for seemingly lost causes and unattainable ideals or longing for bygone ways of life.

The selection of wallpapers, paint colors, American Empire furniture, Old Paris porcelains, and family portraits with which Kitty and her second husband, Irénée May, have filled the house evokes the burnished grandeur of the antebellum south in its various moods. The ground floor rooms, transformed into elegant entertaining chambers, express Victorian formality. The pale salmon walls of the entrance hall provide a perfect foil for a dark mahogany sofa with scrolled arms and blue-black upholstery. A large portrait of one of Irénée's ancestors, Francis Gurney du Pont, who married Charlestonian Eliza Simons, presides above the staircase. The dining room that opens off the hallway offers a playful contrast, with its mural scenes of Italian landscape and architecture. But the English table, Old Paris porcelain, and American Empire sideboard creates a sense of continuity between this room and the next, a large drawing room.

LEFT: Sky blue damask on a French armchair comple- ments the paler shade of blue silk imitated on the panels of wallpaper. Amethyst glass sconces Kitty inherited from her mother flank a circa 1820 overmantel mirror and mid-nineteenth-century lamp.

OPPOSITE: Reproduction wallpaper from Brunschwig & Fils, based on a nineteenth-century pattern in the collection of the Musée des Arts Decoratifs, covers the walls of the bedroom. Delicately proportioned French armchairs and gilded mirrors with swags and bows contribute further to the soft femininity of the master bedroom.

This room, with its crimson wallpaper, dusky furniture, and host of painted ancestors is a perfect archetype of the late-nineteenth-century draw- ing room. "I love walking into a room that looks like nothing has been changed or no one has been there for years," exclaims Kitty. Although all the bronze bibelots and crystal pendants on the chan- delier are perfectly dusted, her Charleston drawing room does feel like a luxuriously decorated time capsule, frozen in a moment in the last decades of the nineteenth century.

Even when Kitty and Irénée are absent, the room is populated by elegant Victorians, including a coquettish lady from New Orleans whose painted visage hangs above the piano and the portrait of a serene young matron holding a child on her lap.

"They have the same dress and hairstyles, but they are so different in personality," Kitty notes. "I always wonder if they like each other, and I don't think they do!" The young mother is believed to be Carolyn Petigru, daughter of James, who may have once sat upon the red and white sofa that is one of three sofas arranged in the parlor.

In the large room above, Kitty transformed what had been a masculine law office filled with books and heavy furniture into an airy bower. With windows on three sides, one of which overlooks the courtyard garden, and pale blue wallpaper and Roman shades, the room feels like an enclosed bit of sky or a fragment of a Fragonard painting. When Kitty discovered the Brunschwig & Fils reproduction of the French wallpaper that came

from the archives of the Musée des Arts Decoratifs, she knew at once she wanted it for her Charleston bedroom. The panels, which depict draped swags of blue silk, fit perfectly into the architectonic moldings of the room, softening the hard edges of square pilasters and cornices.

A fine American table with slender legs stands in the middle of the room, surrounded by up-holstered pieces with feminine, curvilinear lines. An early-nineteenth-century gilded overmantel mirror hangs above the mantel, delicately detailed with a neoclassical frieze. In front of it stands a girandole with a gilded figure of a girl and her dog depicted with a hint of sentimentality. Ivory-topped boxes, jars, and brushes cover the surface of a chest of drawers that is surmounted by a

gilded and garlanded mirror perfect for complet-ing a Victorian toilette.

The garden that lies below the bedroom windows shares the timeless atmosphere of the house. The current residents modified the plantings with the assistance of Charleston-based landscape architect Sheila Wertimer, a favorite among local garden owners, thanks to her familiarity with Charles-ton garden traditions. The Mays also added an antique fountain to what was, in the building's earlier incarnation, a utilitarian yard. The result is a hushed hideaway with mossy brick walls and pav-ings where only the bells of nearby St. Michael's Church disturb the peace, marking the passage of hours just as they did when James Petigru, Susan Pringle Frost, and the three sisters lived there.

OPPOSITE: Bronze d'oré, or gilded bronze, was a favorite material in France and England for light fixtures, the gleaming gold metal and crystal pendants reflecting and refracting the candle's glow. The base of this girandole depicts a charming scene of a young girl embracing her dog.

TOP RIGHT: Antique oil lamps converted for electricity illuminate the top of a chest of drawers where typical nineteenth-century vanity accoutrements ornamented with ivory and monograms sit atop an embroidered linen cloth.

BOTTOM RIGHT: An antique fountain stands in the center of the garden where the steeple of St. Michael's church can be seen and the ringing of its bells heard throughout the day.

CHARLESTON ELEGANCE

A REMODELED NINETEENTH-CENTURY CARRIAGE HOUSE
A Private Residence

The transformation of antique utilitarian buildings into residential quarters became a common practice in post–Civil War-, Reconstruction-, and Depression-Era Charleston, when the city's slave quarters, kitchen and laundry houses, and once-thriving warehouses fell into disuse. But no other transformation has been as successful as that of the former carriage house of the opulent Calhoun Mansion in evoking the grace and elegance of late-eighteenth-century domestic style. Upon entering the petite yet perfectly proportioned entrance hall of the house that stands in a bend of lower Church Street, the impression of Old World refinement and understated splendor is complete.

Antique oriental carpets cover the dark amber planks of polished heart pine floors, and faux-marble veining decorates the baseboards of this space where a staircase rises gracefully to the second floor. Against a wall between two doors outlined with simple Georgian style pilasters, the finest English- and French-made furnishings gleam with gilt. A massive carved giltwood eagle supports a George II console table, surmounted by an eighteenth-century Chippendale mirror with fanciful baroque detailing. Ebonized and gilded French sconces in the form of Egyptian figures flank the mirror, injecting a touch of the early-nineteenth-century Empire style.

It is hard to imagine that horses once trod this space on their way to the stables that once occupied the room now decorated as a library with

OPPOSITE: As it approaches the house, the lawn gives way to a raised, stone terrace decorated with giant eighteenth-century French olive oil urns and jardinières, similar to those used in the gardens of Versailles for citrus trees.

ABOVE: A wrought-iron gate with a pattern of volutes, diminishing in size as they approach the bottom, frames a view of the former stable yard, transformed into a formal garden with symmetrical paths and plantings that mask the irregularity of the plot.

LEFT: The carriage house and its garden occupy a curve in the street, which explains the irregular shapes of the rooms and garden. The placement of windows and doors indicates that the remodeled carriage house now conforms to a classic Georgian double house plan.

OPPOSITE: Eighteenth-century French olive oil urns from Provence and antique jardinières sit on the brick terrace that parallels the drawing and dining rooms. Espaliered camellias create leafy silhouettes on the old brick walls surrounding the garden.

warm cypress walls, a fine antique Serapi carpet, rare books, and artwork. But when this two-story structure was built in 1875, it served as the carriage house for the Calhoun Mansion, a grand Italianate dwelling completed the following year as the home of George Williams (later named for his son-in-law Patrick Calhoun). A banker and a merchant, Williams was one of the New South entrepreneurs of Charleston who hoped to recover the city's antebellum prosperity by introducing new trade patterns and attitudes. The mansion he constructed is Charleston's most opulent late-nineteenth-century dwelling, and the adjacent carriage house and stable yard were quite commodious.

By 1932, the mansion passed out of Williams' hands and the carriage house and stable yard were sold off. Present-day Charlestonians recall playing as children in the empty stalls and haylofts and, later, storing boats in the increasingly dilapidated structure. But in 1939, a wealthy couple from the northeast bought the property, in a trend of well-off northerners

purchasing Charleston houses as winter homes and plantation properties as hunting grounds. According to a history of the carriage house written by Charlestonian David Farrow, the new owners, Mr. and Mrs. Louis Gourd fit this mold.

Citing an interview with Charlestonian Elliott Hutson, Farrow writes: "Louis was quite a sportsman who had some quail properties leased here, there and yonder. . . . He was a sharp dresser, and always had the finest tweeds on and English leather, guns . . ." Hutson continues, describing Louis' wife, Liz, originally from Tuxedo Park, New York. "She was looking for a piece of property to restore, and her eye fell on that piece of property . . ." Mrs. Gourd hired Albert Simons, the foremost architect working in Charleston at the time, to transform the carriage house into a diminutive late-Georgian-style residence.

An article about the final result, published in Charleston's *News and Courier* in 1941, describes

LEFT: The redesigned carriage house is now a diminutive Georgian double house, with four rooms on each floor opening off a central stair hall. The entrance hall features a dramatic George II console table supported by a carved giltwood eagle.

OPPOSITE: A carpet inspired by an eighteenth-century French pattern was selected for the drawing room because its all-over floral pattern helped to mask the room's asymmetry. Reproduction neoclassical style sofas complement an eclectic collection of furniture ranging from a seventeenth-century Chinese Huanghuali chair, a Louis XV clock, and coffee tables made from Chinese export black lacquer panels in the late eighteenth and early nineteenth centuries.

"a dwelling of decided charm marked by delicate woodwork and a curving staircase. The interior which held eight stalls, carriage space, and servants' rooms was removed entirely, except for some of the same flooring. . . . The new interior shows the influence of the architecture of the eighteenth and early nineteenth centuries." This remodeling reflects the mid-twentieth-century Colonial Revival, a movement present-day interior designer Thomas Jayne describes as less colorful and more restrained than the actual period it emulated. "In truth, the eighteenth century was inventive and colorful and had multiple moods, ranging from rustic simplicity to rococo interiors of great beauty and elaboration," he explains. Photographs of the Gourds' interior, published in the 1956 volume, *Southern Interiors of Charleston, South Carolina*, reveals the

twentieth-century restraint Jayne describes. Plain carpets cover the floors in rooms decorated with simply detailed English mahogany furniture, and walls are hung with bird prints and portraits.

When the present-day owner, then a widower, bought the property in 1991, he brought to it a collection of inherited furniture that reflects the much more ebullient character of eighteenth-century English style, including the penchants for baroque and rococo forms borrowed from France and the ornate chinoiserie favored by Chippendale. His collection also included an eclectic selection of French, English, and American art spanning several centuries. To integrate these belongings into a cohesive and elegant interior, he hired Jayne, because of his reputation as a designer deeply versed in the

traditions of eighteenth-century Anglo and Anglo-American design. Jayne at once saw an intriguing parallel between this converted carriage house and English precedents: "In the late eighteenth and nineteenth centuries, people in London closed their houses for the summer and moved some of their furniture to country houses, where you find objects from a much grander house used in a more bucolic setting . . ."

In the case of this carriage house, the bucolic setting is provided by a walled garden visible through French doors located in the main entertaining rooms. When the homeowner remarried in 1995, the wedding took place in this intimate garden. Laid out circa 1940 as a private garden by Margaret Mikell Barnwell, the irregularly shaped space was

originally planted with azaleas, camellias, and flowering peaches, as well as a young live oak tree described as being no larger than a buggy whip. Before long, the tree had grown and spread so much that the one-time sun garden was largely in shade. Subsequent owners of the house hired Charleston's then-favorite landscape architect, Loutrell Briggs, to redesign the garden accordingly. The final form, still intact today, featured a rectangular lawn surrounded by brick walls, paved paths, and espaliered camellias that create a sense of symmetry and enclosure.

Working over a period of several years with the homeowner and his wife, Jayne decided to visually link the house's narrow, rectangular drawing room to this garden. He selected a floral patterned carpet woven in an English atelier and inspired by a

OPPOSITE: A screen covered with rare seventeenth-century tapestry forms the focal point in the dining room, where the restrained cornice moldings and mantel recede into the background. Jayne upholstered the walls with English silk to create a dramatic setting for the screen and the dining room it graces. The silk also provides a perfect foil both for late-nineteenth-century paintings by Jane Peterson and Karl Frederick Frieseke and a pair of marble-topped Irish late-Georgian consoles.

RIGHT: This eighteenth-century portrait by Jeremiah Theus dates from the period which the house's architecture and overall design evoke. Most of the remaining artwork dates from the nineteenth and twentieth centuries, offering what designer Thomas Jayne considers pleasing anachronism. "It immediately relaxes a room to have things not be all of the same period," he notes.

carpet in an eighteenth-century French chateau to create continuity with the garden visible through the room's French doors. The overall pattern of the carpet also helps mask the room's irregular shape. The designer's next challenge was to create an arrangement of furnishings that encouraged sitting and gathering in the long space. To this end, he had two elegant sofas made in reproduction neoclassical style for the room. The homeowners added a Chinese Chippendale chair, a seventeenth-century Chinese Huanghuali chair, and an unmatched pair of coffee tables made from Chinese lacquered screens. "Coffee tables like these, made from the panels of imported screens in the eighteenth and nineteenth centuries, were an American invention," explains one of the residents.

A portrait by renowned Colonial-era portrait artist Jeremiah Theus hangs above one of the sofas. The subject, a genteel Charleston lady named Mrs. Horry, wears pale yellow silk that reflects the room's golden glow, and the rococo frame of gilded wood adds yet another decorative embellishment.

"The formal elegance of this interior is a response to Charleston's tradition of understatement," explains Jayne, "but it is full of occasional flourishes and surprises like that wonderful rococo frame."

This balance of understated elegance and embellishment continues in the dining room, which, in the time of Mrs. Gourd, was painted a subdued shade of antiqued green inspired by Colonial Williamsburg. Jayne suggested upholstering the walls with silk the color of new moss—an opulent touch in keeping with the Georgian luxury. The hue was chosen to complement one of the homeowner's finest heirlooms, a screen of seventeenth-century French tapestry with a floral pattern in shades of deep ruby, gold, and lapis lazuli. A gilt filet surrounds the upholstered walls, and curtains of matching green silk, finished with a French gold-toned trim, hang from the windows. "If you look at the eighteenth-century sources," Jayne explains, "walls covered in fabric or wallpaper always had borders. The gilt reflects the light at night, so when the room is candlelit, you get an underlying shimmer."

TOP LEFT: The reproduction table is set with Steuben water goblets, Baccarat wine glasses, and Steuben teardrop candlesticks, whose crystal matches the glitter of crystal pendant sconces mounted above the fireplace. Plates of Royal Copenhagen Flora Danica china decorated with acorns and roses are arranged between settings of heavy English silver, complementing the rich garden palette of the room.

TOP RIGHT: Sweeping silk draperies and the floral pattern of the seventeenth-century French tapestry screen soften the dining room where Georgian-style paneling, door, and window surrounds create a severe architectural setting.

OPPOSITE: Edwardian-style chairs upholstered in leather provide comfortable seating in the library where books are arrayed in shelves built into the cypress paneling and an early-nineteenth-century circular bookcase.

ABOVE: Decorative arts specialist Thomas Savage advised the homeowner on the renovation of this bathroom, using proportions and materials, including mahogany and Italian marble, that complement the late-Georgian style of the other rooms. A Khotan carpet adds a touch of color, soft texture, and pattern to the room.

OPPOSITE: Designer Thomas Jayne describes the large four-poster bed, with its elaborately draped and decorated canopy, as floating like an island in the center of the bedroom. Lamps with decoupage bases featuring old-fashioned flowers custom-made by Charleston designer Sheila Potter contribute garden notes to the room, as do the silk rosettes on the bed hangings.

OPPOSITE: An American sofa incorporating the shield-back form favored by British designer George Hepplewhite stands before French doors that open onto a shallow iron balcony and are surmounted by a delicately proportioned fanlight.

The residents dine daily in this elegant chamber and frequently host dinner parties here, but their favorite room for informal gatherings is the library that stands across the hall from the formal drawing room. While the drawing room suggests feminine delicacy, the library, with its rich cypress walls and Edwardian style leather armchairs, its hunting trophies and antique English billy clubs, is a more masculine domain. Used as the gun room during the Gourds' residence, this small chamber is now a library-sitting room. With rich, red damask curtains, leather upholstered furnishings, and gilded-leather volumes, it is one of the most inviting spaces in the house, and one that glows with embracing warmth at night.

The very masculine master bathroom on the second floor was designed before the homeowner remarried by then-Charleston-based decorative arts specialist, Tom Savage, who conceived of the mahogany and marble fittings. These contrast with the much more feminine master bedroom, which is dominated by a decorative four-poster bed with fluted polychrome columns. Designed by Jayne, it draws upon the pattern books of Thomas Sheraton and George Hepplewhite, with a nod to John Fowler and Sister Parrish. Because the new lady of the house studied horticulture and has a passion for flowers, blue silk rosettes were incorporated into the elaborately draped canopy and a floral pattern chosen for the room's curtains. Overlooking the garden from its windows, surrounded by the branches of the old live oak tree, and bathed in the sound of splashing fountains from the Calhoun Mansion's grounds next door, the room feels like yet another extension of what the homeowners call "the most beguiling little garden in Charleston."

THE CAPERS MOTTE SMITH HOUSE
The Home of Ellen and Dan Kiser

Charleston's preservation movement began in the 1920s, when its grand Georgian and Federal houses began to fall prey to a combination of dilapidation, demolition, and architectural scavenging. At that time, several prominent houses were torn down to make room for gas stations and other modern structures, and others witnessed the removal of their antique decorative details. "The town has found it had to protect itself from collectors of everything from ironwork to complete houses," wrote Samuel Gaillard Stoney in his 1944 volume, *This is Charleston*, which catalogued many of the city's finest buildings.

Alice Ravenel Huger Smith, an artist and preservationist, contributed her own volume recording Charleston's threatened architecture three decades early, with the 1917 publication of *The Dwelling Houses of Charleston*. Among the houses she described is the circa 1745 Georgian double house on Meeting Street where she was born and where she died in 1959, survived by a sister who lived on in the house for another decade. They were the second generation of Smiths to live in the fine dwelling house, whose residents also included eighteenth-century Charlestonian Jacob Motte, treasurer of the crown colony and one of the richest men in America.

During Motte's residence, from 1759 to 1770, the house still maintained its original mid-Georgian style appearance, with a nearly square brick façade and center-hall entrance surrounded by short rectangular windows. This façade was significantly

OPPOSITE: Built circa 1745, this classic Georgian double house was restored to its original configuration in the 1970s, when a Charleston single-house-style piazza added in the nineteenth century was removed.

ABOVE: One of the house's several illustrious residents included Charleston Renaissance artist Alice Ravenel Huger Smith. A watercolor by the artist (not seen) inspired the dining room's blue-green shade. A painting by fellow Charleston Renaissance artist, Alfred Hutty, is reflected in the mirror.

TOP LEFT: Much of the house's original cypress Georgian paneling is intact, as seen in this drawing room. One of the house's Federal period owners added stylish early-nineteenth-century details, including this mantel decorated with composition detail.

BOTTOM LEFT: The previous residents of the house made efforts to restore the house to its original Georgian appearance, replacing the center hall to its initial position (it had been removed to create a double parlor in the nineteenth century). They also stripped paint from much of the cypress paneling, leaving its warm grain bare in this drawing room.

OPPOSITE: English porcelain herons stand upon the dining room table, evoking the low-country flora and fauna that inspired many of Smith's paintings.

altered by O'Brien Smith, an early-nineteenth-century owner who is credited with adding a piazza on the southeastern façade of the house and eliminating a portion of the center hall to link the two front rooms into a double parlor. This same owner also elongated the house's windows to conform to Federal style proportions and installed four mantels with composition detail designed by the firm of Ramage & Ferguson. This Scottish firm exported a number of mantel decorations to Charleston with motifs ranging from typical neoclassical garlands and urns to elaborate scenes of figures and natural elements.

"This house is a very good example of the strong reaction in this country against things Georgian," explains current resident, Ellen Kiser. "After the Revolution, it was purged of Georgian detail and made to look like a dwelling of the new republic." Even so, English tastes still subtly prevailed, since the Federal style mimicked aesthetics then popular in England, and much of the original Georgian cypress wall paneling and cornice moldings remained. By the time Smith's grandmother bought the house following the Civil War, it was described as being in "ruinous condition." The Smiths, however, were careful custodians of its architectural glory, making it possible for later residents to conduct successful restoration projects.

The first of these took place in the 1970s, when the couple who purchased the house removed the piazza and restored the center hall arrangements of rooms. These residents also removed layers of

OPPOSITE: The ballroom's cypress paneling is painted a warm gold, a shade that paint analysis revealed was formerly used in the room. A portrait by Thomas Sully, III, great-great-great-grandson of the renowned American nineteenth-century portrait painter, hangs above a Steinway grand piano.

TOP RIGHT: A Fisk pipe organ nearly fills a room opening off the ballroom, where eleven-foot ceilings easily accommodate its graceful form. Present resident, Dan Kiser, one-time assistant organist at Yale University, frequently plays upon it. Another Sully portrait hangs on the wall.

BOTTOM RIGHT: Morning sun illuminates the fine details of a classical figure rendered in composition, a mixture of glue and other ingredients that forms resilient relief decoration when shaped in molds.

interior paint and replaced missing elements of the second floor ballroom's Georgian detail. By the time Ellen and her husband Dan Kiser bought the house in 1998, it once more resembled its original stately Georgian configuration, but still required substantial repairs and renovation.

The Kisers purchased the house with a strong spirit of preservation. In addition to completing the restoration of the house and its dependencies, they also placed easements on it—legal documents that protect the property in perpetuity. These include easements protecting the exterior of the building and the interior of all rooms except bathrooms and the kitchen; one preventing subdivision of the large lot; and one precluding residents from operating it as a bed and breakfast. Arranged through Historic Charleston Foundation, such easements give the organization authority to regulate future modifications in order to protect Charleston's built environment.

"We just thought it was the right thing to do," says Dan. "We have done what we hope is a sensitive restoration of the house, and we want it to be treated that way in the future." In order to insure that their restoration was appropriate to the historic house, the Kisers worked for three years with restoration architect Richard Marks. Combining early experience in the building trades in Charleston with studies at the University of Pennsylvania, Marks brought decades of wisdom, as well as passion, to the project. "When we discovered a large egg-shaped cistern near the kitchen, Richard just climbed right into it and started digging with his hands," Ellen recalls.

One of Marks' most noticeable contributions to the property is a glass and wood hyphen-like addition that connects the main house with the kitchen dependency behind it. This outbuilding, once housing a kitchen, laundry, and servants' quarters, had never been connected to the house. The previous residents used it as a bed and breakfast, transforming one of the rooms of the original house into a kitchen. Marks' addition allowed the Kisers to restore the kitchen house to its intended purpose. Because the addition's walls and ceiling are glazed, it is possible to stand in the small space and still imagine the separation between house and its

dependency. The addition is also designed in such a way that future generations wishing to restore the space between the two buildings can do so without damaging them.

The Kisers remodeled the dependency to include a large kitchen, floored with unglazed tile (rather than dirt or brick, which would be more to the period), cabinets made from old pine salvaged from a South Carolina barn, and counters of soapstone, a material that would have been in use in the period. This room and the adjoining guest quarters are the most informal spaces in the house. All of the main structure's rooms are far more opulent, with walls covered with cypress paneling and crowned with neoclassical moldings. Each window is draped with lavishly trimmed curtains and every room is deco-

rated with fine American or English antiques.

To decorate the dining room that opens off the center hall, the Kisers bought several paintings from the Charleston Renaissance era, a period in the 1920s and 30s when the city was home to a talented group of local and visiting artists, including Alice Ravenel Huger Smith. A watercolor of lush local scenery by Smith hangs above the dining room's mantel and inspired the room's cool blue-green shade. A pair of English porcelain herons stand on the dining room table, complementing the glade-like color of the room.

The drawing room across the hall features some of the Kisers' finest antiques, including an American sofa in the classical taste, made circa 1815–1830. Its

OPPOSITE: The Kisers returned the kitchen house to its original function. Cabinetry custom-made from antique pine salvaged from a South Carolina barn and a gaso-lier-style lighting fixture give the room old-fashioned charm.

TOP RIGHT: Landscape designer Jan Frazee divided the Kisers' long garden into a series of rooms, beginning with this parterre garden adjacent to the main house and two-story kitchen dependency. The Kisers often enjoy meals in this space, surrounded by the tall podocarpus yew hedge, low boxwood parterres, and old camellias.

BOTTOM RIGHT: Brick pillars covered with stucco sup-port the piazza that runs the length of the dependency which originally housed a kitchen, laundry, and servants quarters. Operated as a bed and breakfast in the 1970s, it now serves as the Kisers' kitchen and private guest quarters.

TOP LEFT: A neoclassical bronze figure stands in the middle of the secret garden where green plants with a variety of leaf shapes and textures create visual interest.

TOP MIDDLE: The house's service wing overlooks a secret garden that Frazee created by planting a tall hedge of podocarpus yew trees separating this small shade garden from the adjacent parterre garden.

TOP RIGHT: The old brick walls of the original carriage house still stand at the back of the property. Stairs lead down to a sunken garden that changes appearance with the seasons as Ellen experiments with different plantings.

period-style silk damask upholstery with stripes of ruby and gold gave the room its color scheme. Other notable antiques in the room include the girandole mirror over the mantel, a bull's eye mirror with gilded candlearms made in London, circa 1790–1806. While the architectonic moldings above the mantel are Georgian in style, the delicate composition detail on the mantel itself, made by Ramage & Ferguson, was added in the Federal period.

"We find that the more grandly proportioned furnishings of the Federal period tend to look better in this house than eighteenth-century pieces," notes Dan. These also include the drawing room's circa 1830 drum table, a game table in the center of the room labeled John Needles, who was Baltimore's leading cabinetmaker in the early nineteenth century, and an American secretary bookcase. The chandelier and a large copy of an Old Master painting depicting John the Baptist are the only continental European elements in the room.

Ellen designed curtains for this, and all the other rooms, drawing inspiration from books about period styles and visits to historic houses in the British Isles and America, including the Winterthur Museum. "I love going to estate sales and auctions and finding treasures," says Ellen, who has made an informal study of furniture craftsmanship and details. One of the things that attracted her to this house was its many rooms awaiting furnishing and its seventy-five windows in need of curtains. She also liked the fact that the tall ceilings would accommodate a Fisk pipe organ, located in the second floor ballroom. Ellen and her husband met while studying pipe organ at the Yale University School of Music, and Dan still plays regularly on the organ.

An avid gardener, Ellen was also intrigued by the lot itself, which measures fifty-four by three hundred feet and is surrounded by tall brick walls. The Kisers recently redesigned the garden with the help of Winter Park, Florida landscape designer, Jan Frazee. "In the original configuration of the garden, you could stand at one end and see all the way to the other, including the 1970s swimming pool in the middle," says Ellen. The landscape designer devised a series of rooms including a brick terrace immediately behind the house which terminates in a tall yew hedge. Forming a dark green backdrop for a triple-tiered fountain, the hedge also blocks the view into the rest of the garden.

A secret garden lies hidden on the far side of the hedge, as well as the bricked pool terrace, a pergola, and a walled garden at the back of the property that includes the original walls of the carriage house. "We considered removing the pool," says Dan. But by replastering the lining in a dark shade of gray, the Kisers succeeded in transforming it into a reflecting pool, thus minimizing its contemporary intrusion upon the old world space.

"The property has a lot of original materials that we did not want to lose: the brick walls and old brick pavings, the privies, the carriage house walls, and many old plants," comments Dan. The Kisers selected Frazee from several potential designers because she devised a creative plan that preserved these details, including an array of mature camellias, tea olives, hollies and boxwoods. "Jan found a way of creating beautiful spaces with all those things worked into the plan," he adds. As a result, the garden now shares the same spirit that infuses the house: a passion for preservation and an understanding that the gifts of the past are to be cherished, not taken for granted or cast away.

OPPOSITE: Two brick privies with Gothic-style doors stand on the property. They now flank an oval swimming pool, added in the 1970s. The pool's terrace of old brick and dark gray plaster color help to minimize its anachronistic appearance.

ABOVE: Cool blue hydrangeas border one side of the oval swimming pool that is surrounded by a hardscape of old brick. Ellen found the wooden sculpture of a porpoise in an antiques shop, purchasing it as a reminder of the porpoises that swim in the waters surrounding Charleston's Battery.

THE TIMOTHY FORD HOUSE
The Home of Helen and Bert Pruitt

A tall, white single house stands on Meeting Street with an iron fence entangled with the most famous wisteria vine in Charleston. The antique plant was memorialized in 1927 by American artist Childe Hassam, who came to winter in Charleston. He and other visiting and local artists spawned a movement known as the Charleston Renaissance that celebrated the region's old-world beauty and air of romantic decay. The vine is still admired each spring by locals and visitors who come to visit the city's houses and gardens in annual tours arranged by Historic Charleston Foundation. Its cascades of silvery violet blooms serve as an invitation to pause, gaze through the fence, and step out of time into Charleston's timeless tradition of hospitality.

Before the city's tourist population swelled in recent decades, it was common for Charlestonians to leave their gates ajar as a sign that their garden was open to visitors. Today, tourists must wait for invitations, but Charleston gardens still spill their bounty over the tops of brick and iron walls, issuing tantalizing glimpses of the beauty that lies beyond. Springtime passersby of the Timothy Ford house are treated not only to the sight and subtly sweet scent of the wisteria, but also to the glory of flowering cherry trees that rise above the vine-clad boundary.

These double Japanese Kwanzan cherries were planted more than a quarter of a century ago to celebrate the debut of long-time residents Bert and Helen Pruitt's eldest daughter. The event also occasioned the construction of a bell-shaped gazebo, inspired by one designed by Russell Page for the Duchess of Beaufort in England. Its white trellised walls are a perfect foil for the mossy brick wall and path that hug the garden's southeast boundary. During parties, the gazebo provides graceful shelter for guests who gather to share champagne, cocktails, tea, or conversation.

The house, built in 1800 for Timothy Ford, a prominent lawyer whose friends included George Washington and the Marquis de Lafayette, is ideal for entertaining. The Marquis was its most famous guest, coming to visit Mr. Ford in 1824. The rooms he then visited probably did not greatly differ in appearance from the ones inhabited today by the Pruitts, both South Carolinians with an instinct for Charleston style. "I've always joked that I meant to be born in Charleston, but I needed to be close to my mother that day," says Helen, who, like her husband, was born in the upstate cotton capital of Anderson.

The house still retains its original cypress paneling, cornice moldings, and mantels, with original gougework and composition detail also well preserved. Although these elements were obscured beneath more than a dozen layers of paint when the Pruitts bought the house, they were able to strip them and restore them to their crisp, early-Federal silhouettes. "The house is decorated in a very restrained Federal style," Helen comments, noting that in many aspects, the house more closely resembles late Georgian houses in the neighborhood.

Helen selected a jade-green shade from the Colonial Williamsburg palette for the moldings in the first floor drawing room, painting their neoclassical reliefs in contrasting white. This color scheme matches that of a jasperware tea set she received as a wedding gift from her husband, then commander

of an air force hospital in England. Invented by Thomas Wedgwood in 1775, jasperware features white-robed Grecian forms gracefully poised on a matte ground of green, lavender, blue, and even black. Inspired by the architectural motifs then popular, jasperware was all the rage in late-eighteenth- and early-nineteenth-century England and America.

Swags of crimson draperies hang from the drawing room's windows, where louvered wooden blinds filter the light, as they would have in the early nineteenth century. A mix of English and American furniture graces the room, accented in classic Charleston style by Asian decorative objects, including Chinese porcelains. "All my life, I've loved Chinese things," says Helen. "The English did, too, because they had such a huge China trade," she adds. "My ancestors are as Scots and English and Welsh as you can get, so I guess this penchant is just a little bit genetic."

The dining room that lies across the house's center hall offers an even purer expression of late Georgian and Federal tastes. Cypress wainscoting and cornice moldings detailed with dentil and triglyph patterns borrowed from temple architecture crown the walls. A magnificent sideboard of highly grained mahogany inlaid with satinwood, made in Charleston circa 1790, stands against one wall.

PREVIOUS PAGE: A double piazza shades the southeastern façade of the Timothy Ford house, built in 1800. Situated to capture the prevailing breezes from the nearby harbor, this piazza also provides the perfect vantage point from which to enjoy the garden below.

OPPOSITE: A stand of double Japanese Kwanzan cherry trees transforms the front garden room into a bower of pink blossoms each spring. The piazza is furnished with a joggling board, an old-fashioned bench with a springy seat balanced on rocking legs.

Polished silver vessels cover its surface, as well as that of a mid-eighteenth-century English table surrounded by Chippendale chairs. A collection of Chinese export ware, including several pieces from Nanking and a variety of blue Canton patterns, are displayed to advantage in a niche painted dark gold. This type of china was widely collected by eighteenth- and nineteenth-century Charlestonians, who purchased it from British merchants engaged in the China trade

Asian art covers the walls, including Chinese watercolors painted on silk, a portrait of a Korean monk, and a selection of antique Persian miniatures the Pruitts bought on a trip to Iran in the 1970s. Such imports and souvenirs of Eastern travel became popular in Charleston in the late nineteenth and twentieth centuries, when Americans enjoyed direct trade and tourism with the East. An ornate cabinet carved of Indian teak, which the Pruitts purchased in England, reflects Victorian English tastes (Queen Victoria had a similar one in her Kensington Palace apartments).

OPPOSITE: Sharply pruned hedges of boxwood form wall-like hedges separating the "rooms" of the Pruitts' garden. Their glossy green leaves provide dark contrast with the pink blossoms of cherry trees, azaleas, and camellias.

TOP RIGHT: Loutrell Briggs laid out this parterre garden before 1936, using broken oyster shell instead of brick for the walkways. Azaleas surround four old camellias in each corner and a large elm tree stands in one corner.

BOTTOM RIGHT: The wisteria-laden iron fence casts a shadow on the carpet of green grass in the front of the Pruitts' garden, which is surrounded by a selection of trees and shrubs that bloom year-round.

TOP LEFT: The Pruitts' love of pairing Asian decorative elements with English and American antiques reveals a natural penchant for eighteenth- and nineteenth-century Charleston style. This formal drawing room retains original cypress moldings painted in shades of green and white inspired by Wedgwood jasperware.

BOTTOM LEFT: The Pruitts found this Victorian carved Indian teak chest in England—a vestige of the days when India was the jewel in the crown of Britain's empire. A similar chest stands in Queen Victoria's apartments in Kensington Palace. An Ichibana arrangement of purple irises in a Chinese boat-shaped container adds another exotic element to the tableau.

OPPOSITE: After the Pruitts removed fourteen layers of paint, the delicate gougework along the top of the dining room mantel became visible. Helen painted the areas of deepest relief in a Colonial Williamsburg shade called Tobacco to accentuate the decorative detail. A fine 1890 Charleston-made sideboard features oval panels of highly grained mahogany and bands of satinwood inlay.

Ichibana floral arrangements decorate the rooms, indicating yet another aspect of Helen's Asia-mania. Although Ichibana is a Japanese form, Helen explains, it derives from Chinese paintings and literary traditions and uses containers based on Chinese models, including the barque, or carved boat, that holds purple irises in the dining room.

During parties, guests enter the house through the piazza, passing by the colorful garden on the way into the house's entertaining rooms. In the springtime and fall, parties often take place on the piazzas, with guests sipping cool drinks while enjoying the scent of gardenias and magnolias. From this vantage point, they can best appreciate the design of the garden, which is divided into room-like spaces in traditional formal English style.

Circular motifs visually unite the three spaces, with a round lawn in the center of the front garden

room, surrounded by cherry trees, Korean boxwood, azaleas, and camellias—all Asian cultivars. The middle room of the garden features a brick parterre laid out in a rose-window design, with a large whetstone that belonged to Helen's grandfather in the center. The rear garden was designed by Loutrell Briggs, Charleston's mid-twentieth-century garden designer of choice and an expert in early American garden styles. This square space includes four large camellias in each corner with a knot-like planting of boxwood parterres in its center.

More naturalistic plantings edge these three rooms with a large elm tree and tea olives providing shade over brick paths lined with ginger lilies and shade-loving plants. Fragrant white confederate jasmine climbs the gazebo and yellow Carolina jasmine clings to an iron arch, offering star-shaped blooms as highlights against the dark green foliage. Along this edge of the garden, where fountains burble and moss grows against the brick wall, the Pruitts and their guests enjoy the benediction of shade on even the brightest summer day.

Whether sitting in their gazebo, dining in Federal surroundings, or enjoying tea on their second floor piazza, the Pruitts make full use of this historic residence and share it liberally with family, friends, and even strangers during public tours. "We love this house, and she has loved us," says Helen. "We like to share her, and we've tried our best to care for her so that she can be enjoyed by the next generation to come along."

ABOVE Piazza set for tea: The second floor piazza is furnished in old-fashioned Charleston style with painted wicker, bright green ferns, and Chinese decorative objects. The Pruitts often enjoy tea together on its shaded, breezy expanse.

TOP RIGHT: The Pruitts commissioned this gazebo, designed after one in the garden of the Duchess of Beaufort, on the occasion of their eldest daughter's debut. Since then, it has been the site of countless parties as well as private gatherings with family and friends.

BOTTOM RIGHT: For a small tea party, Helen's Wedgwood jasperware tea set graces a damask- and lace-clad table set beneath the white latticework of the garden gazebo.

Resource Guide

This guide includes contact information for the architectural and design professionals and decorative arts resources cited in this book.

Architects, Preservation Consultants, and Contractors

W. G. Clark, architect
434.872.9499
www.wgclark-architects.com

Beau Clowney, architect
843-722-2040
www.beauclowney.com

Samuel Furr, architect
843-559-5524

JMO Woodworks
843-577-7352
jmowood@bellsouth.net

Glenn Keyes, architect
843-722-4100
www.rgkarchitects.com

John Laurens, preservation consultant
843-723-1746
johnlaurens@bellsouth.net

Richard Marks, restoration consultant/contractor
843-853-0024

Landscape Architects and Garden Designers

Jan Frazee, landscape designer
407-671-9775
jtfrazee@earthlink.net

Eugene G. Johnson, garden designer
843-723-4668
egj111@bellsouth.net

Sheila Wertimer, landscape architect
843-577-3360
www.wertimer.com

Interior Design and Decorative Arts Consultants

Paula Adams, interior designer
843-402-6820

Merrill Benfield Design and Decoration
843-723-1824
mbdesign1@gmail.com

James Evans, interior designer
843-723-7679
liz@margaretdonaldsoninteriors.com

Amelia T. Handegan Interior Design
843-722-9373
amelia@athid.com

Thomas Jayne, interior designer
212-838-9080
www.thomasjaynestudio.com

Vangie Rainsford, decorative arts/antiques consultant
843-723-6302
erainsford@aol.com

Kathleen Rivers Interior Design
843-723-5744
kriversdesign@comcast.net

Sherry Taylor, interior designer
843-723-0575
christianmichi@bellsouth.net

Paints and Wallpapers

Brunschwig & Fils
914-684-5800
www.brunschwig.com

Colors of Historic Charleston
Duron Paints and Wallcoverings
www.duron.com
and
Sherwin Williams
www.sherwin-williams.com

de Gournay
212-564-9750
www.degournay.com

Monuments of Paris wallpaper
Produced by The Twigs
800-824-4204
Also available through
Ernie Gaspard and Assoc.
404-233-8645
www.erniegaspard.com

Williamsburg paint colors
Martin Senour
www.martinsenour.com

Textiles

Scalamandré
www.scalamandre.com

Lulan Artisans
843-722-0118
www.lulan.com

Fine Artists and Decorative Painters

Marty Whaley Adams
The Wells Gallery
843-853-3233

Douglas Balentine
843-722-1797
www.jdouglasbalentine.com

Kristen Bunting
843-830-3373
kristenbunting@comcast.net

Thomas Sully
843-906-3521
www.thomassully.com

Reproduction Furnishings and Tableware

Historic Charleston Foundation licensees, including
Baker Furniture's Historic Charleston Collection,
Mottahedeh's Bourbon Sprig pattern, and others:
Historic Charleston Foundation Reproductions Shop:
843-723-8292
www.historiccharleston.org

Antique Shows, Museums, and Event Venues

Charleston International Antiques Show
843-722-3405
www.historiccharleston.org

The William Aiken House
843-853-1810
www.thewilliamaikenhouse.com

Middleton Place
843-556-6020
www.middletonplace.org

Nathaniel Russell House
843-724-8481
www.historiccharleston.org

Wortham House Bed and Breakfast
843-723-4668
www.bbonline.com/sc/wortham

Index